HITCHCOCK'S NORTH BY NORTHWEST

Hitchcock's North by Northwest: *The Man Who Had Too Much*
© 2013 James Stratton. All Rights Reserved.

No part of this book may be reproduced in any form or by any means, electronic, mechanical, digital, photocopying or recording, except for the inclusion in a review, without permission in writing from the publisher.

Published in the USA by:
BearManor Media
PO Box 1129
Duncan, Oklahoma 73534-1129
www.bearmanormedia.com

ISBN 978-1-59393-245-9

Printed in the United States of America.
Book design by Brian Pearce | Red Jacket Press.

HITCHCOCK'S NORTH BY NORTHWEST

THE MAN WHO HAD TOO MUCH

JAMES STRATTON

TABLE OF CONTENTS

ACKNOWLEDGMENTS 9
1: DOWN THE RABBIT HOLE 13
2: PERFORMANCE ANXIETY 17
3: CLOCK WORK 27
4: VISUAL UNITY 35
5: NORTH BY NOTORIOUS 45
6: OTHER IDENTIFIED OBJECTS 53
7: HANDS DOWN 57
8: MYTH 63
9: NEW YORK, NEW YORK 69
10: A DRINKING LIFE 73
11: MUM 77
12: EVA/EVE 83
13: VANDAMMED 93
14: WHAT ABOUT LEONARD? 97
15: SPY vs. SPY 101
16: "A CARY GRANT PICTURE" 105
17: THE SUIT 111
18: "DUSTIN' CROPS" 115
19: "VALUABLE PROPERTY" 137

20: "THE MAN ON LINCOLN'S NOSE"	143
21: FANDANGO	149
22: AUTRE AUTEUR	157
23: TWO TRAINS RUNNING	163
24: ARS GRATIA ARTIS	167
25: FINALE	173
Appendix A: ROGER THORNHILL'S APPOINTMENTS	179
Appendix B: THE SHOOT	181
Appendix C: CREDITS	185
WORKS CITED	187
INDEX	191

To Roberto
por todo

ACKNOWLEDGMENTS

It all starts somewhere. I would like to thank Richard Stratton for taking me to see my first Hitchcock film and Jan Denman for nurturing a love of books and movies. I am grateful to Robert Bertholf for setting the standard and to both Serafina Bathrick and Joanne McGee for their support and encouragement over many years. Thanks also to Susan Boyd for her special interest in the completion of this book. Susan, Bill Boyd, Chris DeFaria and David Sagal went to bat for me at a critical moment and I would like to express my most sincere gratitude to each of them.

Robin Cresto deserves special thanks for her outstanding work in preparing the manuscript. She is a much-valued friend and colleague. Ben Ohmart and Sandy Grabman at BearManor Media made the finished project actually happen and I am grateful to both for their enthusiasm, support and professionalism. A major thank you to editors Pat Hanson and Wes Britton whose revisions and suggestions helped to shape the final manuscript. In addition, my very strong appreciation goes to Brian Pearce for his creativity and artistry in designing the book.

I cannot say enough about how helpful Matt Severson has been. He opened countless doors for me and strengthened the work with his advice and ideas. I treasure his friendship.

All photos courtesy the Collections of the Margaret Herrick Library. All rights related to the film are reserved by Warner Bros. Entertainment, Inc. All photographic frame enlargements from North by Northwest used with permission of Warner Bros. Entertainment, Inc.

Parenthetical notations of authors and/or page numbers refer to the Works Cited section at the end of the book. I am grateful to those sources for information and insight.

A final note: the chapters may be read in any order determined by reader interest. Sequential order, while recommended, is not required. As such, there is occasionally a restatement of names and plot details between chapters.

*I am but mad north-north-west; when the wind is
southerly I know a hawk from a handsaw.*

HAMLET

1: DOWN THE RABBIT HOLE

If charming and affluent advertising executive James Blandings had not married Myrna Loy and moved to Connecticut to build his dream house, he would have remained in Manhattan and become effortlessly successful advertising executive Roger O. Thornhill. He would have married and, in fairly rapid succession, divorced Dina Merrill and Suzy Parker. He would have secured all the best accounts and would quickly have become a partner in his firm. Dining regularly at Le Moal and Twenty-One, he would attend opening night of *Wonderful Town*, read Murray Kempton in the *Post*, give his Metropolitan Opera tickets to clients and probably have stopped by the Stork Club to hear Manny Balestrero on bass. The initials "R.O.T." would be monogrammed on his white dress shirts, his white handkerchiefs, his fountain pen and his matchbooks. He would weekend in the Hamptons and vacation in Europe. And then suddenly one day — because this is a Hitchcock cautionary tale cum thriller and not an H.C. Potter comedy — he would be punished for all of it.

In fact, Cary Grant, as Roger Thornhill, in *North by Northwest*, is physically abused more than any other actor in Hitchcock's films. No one else comes close. He is kidnapped, force fed a bottle of bourbon, placed nearly unconscious behind the wheel of a brakeless car careening down a cliffside highway, fingered for a murder he didn't commit, pursued as a wanted man aboard the Twentieth-Century Limited, strafed by a cropdusting plane, menaced at an art auction, punched in the face by a forest ranger, held at gunpoint by an evil housekeeper and chased to the edge of Mount Rushmore where a sadistic personal secretary stomps on his fingers as he dangles precariously above the abyss. He is the male predecessor to Melanie Daniels. Both characters are elegant socialites who are roughed up and wised up by forces beyond the gravitational pull of their privilege and influence.

Thornhill's only real transgression is bad karma, comeuppance for feeling too comfortable and secure. Like Henry Fonda in *The Wrong Man*, he is mistaken for someone else, but whereas *The Wrong Man* suggests the bureaucratic torment of Kafka's *The Trial*, *North by Northwest* is closer to the absurdist delirium of "The Hunger Artist" and Lewis Carroll. By signaling for a telegram messenger at just the wrong moment in the Plaza Hotel's Oak Room bar, Thornhill is confused for someone who does not even exist and then swept up in a nightmarish whirlwind of compounding coincidences and assaults that hover between the ridiculous and the terrifying.

Causality links the fantastic episodes of Thornhill's farce but logic does not. Because he answers a page meant for imaginary intelligence agency decoy George Kaplan, Thornhill is abducted and interrogated in a mansion owned by Lester Townsend but commandeered by spymaster Phillip Vandamm. Because he searches out the real Lester Townsend, Thornhill triggers Townsend's murder and gets implicated as the murderer himself. In fleeing the police, Thornhill sneaks aboard a Chicago bound train and finds protection and love in Eve Kendall's sleeping compartment. Bound by the imperatives of a double agent posing as Vandamm's mistress, Eve must send Thornhill into the prairie for a crop-dusting biplane attack even though she loves him. And finally, because he learns that Eve's betrayal was just part of her job, Thornhill follows her to Mount Rushmore and plucks her from the edge of a cliff located somewhere beneath George Washington's chin.

So, yes, the jigsaw pieces fit together, but the image they form is still a garbled hieroglyph. As mimesis, *North by Northwest* is outlandish and preposterous. Authorities are not so easily eluded, beautiful double agents don't materialize on a train randomly chosen for escape and ultramodern hideouts are not constructed within climbing distance of Mount Rushmore. As contemporary morality tale, however, *North by Northwest* is resonantly effective.

In trying to decipher his nightmare and prove his innocence, Thornhill, like Richard Hannay in *The 39 Steps*, sets off on a rambling journey that takes him from New York to Chicago to South Dakota, moving continuously in the northwesterly direction of the film's title. Along the way, Thornhill's sojourn accrues the archetypal narrative patterns and the character revelations of a quest. While finding answers to the Kaplan mystery, Thornhill also finds his better self. He changes from a smug manipulator of others to a caring human being open to the redemptive power of love. With Thornhill as exemplum, *North by Northwest* counsels authentic action over performance, humility over hubris.

North by Northwest is also one of Alfred Hitchcock's most profitable and popular films. Working at M-G-M on the threshold of his sixtieth birthday and given his largest budget to date, Hitchcock fills his fiftieth film with all the insight, skill and technique he developed in a directorial career that began in 1926. On hand to assist is his most familiar and talented production team: cinematographer Robert Burks, editor George Tomasini and composer Bernard Herrmann (the same collaborators who together are also responsible for the second *The Man Who Knew Too Much*, *The Wrong Man*, *Vertigo*, *The Birds* and *Marnie*). There are a sharpness to the Technicolor photography and a precision to the rear projections present to such degree in almost no other Hitchcock production. Location exteriors and studio inserts are blended seamlessly, and the detailed montage of set pieces like the crop-dusting ambush and the Mount Rushmore chase are textbook lessons in how to pace and control viewer responses. As always, Herrmann's score complements this pacing with its unique tempos and cadences — the resounding timpani of the opening credits and the finale, the lively triple meter fandango chases, the melodic oboe-clarinet love theme for Thornhill and Eve Kendall. Every aspect of *North by Northwest* sparkles with a technical confidence and a joy in making movies. The film moves like a sleek modern machine, like the Twentieth-Century Limited Thornhill rides to and from Chicago.

A compendium of his entire work, *North by Northwest* bursts with references to other Hitchcock films. The basic plot is an amalgam of *Notorious* and *The 39 Steps*. The mother-son dynamic humorously echoes *Notorious* and *Strangers on a Train* and prefigures *Psycho* and *The Birds*. Vandamm, the urbane villain, has counterparts in Alex Sebastian of *Notorious* and Uncle Charlie of *Shadow of a Doubt*. Eva Marie Saint's dangerous blonde heroine invites comparison with Grace Kelly, Janet Leigh, Kim Novak and Tippi Hedren. And the life-changing train journey appears in countless films including most notably *The Lady Vanishes* and *Strangers on a Train*. Everything Hitchcock has learned about framing and camera movement is used to full effect — point of view shots to build audience identification with Thornhill, the subjective tracking camera to invade forbidden space, extreme facial close-ups to shock and surprise.

Dismissed as lightly likeable upon its release by many critics and even today by some, *North by Northwest* has been consistently underestimated because it is so much fun to watch. But *North by Northwest* is merely an entertainment in the way that a Graham Greene novel like *The Ministry of Fear* is merely an entertainment; both are pleasurable to experience yet also illuminating on matters of class, culture and society. Reflecting

America's image of itself in the mid twentieth century, Hitchcock's film has much to say about consumerism, gender, politics, urbanization, fashion and fine art. It radiates with dazzling images and gleaming surfaces at the same time that it probes uncertainties behind the spectacle.

At the 32nd Academy Awards (for films released in 1959), *North by Northwest* was nominated for best original screenplay, best editing and best color art direction. In this, the year of the big *Ben-Hur* juggernaut, it won nothing. Doing a much better job of recognizing its importance, the American Film Institute ranked *North by Northwest* number 40 in its 1998 list of the top 100 American films made to that point. Criteria included popularity over time, historical significance and cultural impact. In the 2007 update, *North by Northwest* was number 55. Compensating somewhat for the Oscar slight, *Ben-Hur* was ranked 72nd and 100th in the two different lists. AFI's list of the top 100 "heart-pounding movies in American cinema," published in 2001, has *North by Northwest* at number four; five of the top 20 films on that particular list are directed by Hitchcock. As a critical starting point here, I believe that *North by Northwest* is a genuine masterpiece by a major filmmaker at the height of his artistic powers, and I place it unhesitatingly alongside *Notorious*, *Vertigo*, *Psycho* and *The Birds*. More layered and nuanced than its undisputed entertainment value might otherwise suggest, *North by Northwest* merits the repeat viewings and detailed analysis allotted Hitchcock's finest work.

2: PERFORMANCE ANXIETY

Like the spectacularly theatrical Hamlet, Roger Thornhill uses his talent as an actor to navigate many of the challenges in his life, sometimes out of convenient habit and sometimes out of necessity. In fact, all of the major characters in *North by Northwest* — Thornhill, the Professor, Phillip Vandamm, Eve Kendall — participate in an interlocking series of charades that drive the narrative and that indicate important changes in the situational balance of power.

References to acting and to performing abound throughout the film with characters continually calling each other out for playacting rather than telling the truth. Dexterity in switching roles and in authoring scenarios measures the control one character wields over the others. To demand a performance, to pull the strings of a production, is to gain momentary advantage in this absurdist game of espionage but to transcend the behavioral expectations mandated by specific political, social and economic roles is to become a fully realized human being capable of free agency and empathy for others. Whether Roger Thornhill can achieve this awareness and independence is ultimately much more significant than whether he can retrieve the microfilm from inside Vandamm's Tarascan Warrior statuette.

Although the performance motif is central to how *North by Northwest* constructs its message, it is not alone among Hitchcock's films in referencing role playing and theatricality. In *Vertigo*, Judy Barton (Kim Novak) portrays Madeleine Elster for the benefit of Scottie Ferguson (James Stewart) in a plot by the real Madeleine's husband to murder her for insurance money. Sam Loomis (John Gavin) and Lila Crane (Vera Miles) pretend to be a married couple in *Psycho* in order to search the motel run by Norman Bates (Anthony Perkins), who pulls off a stunning drag performance himself. Creating the "meet cute" which opens *The Birds*, Melanie Daniels (Tippi Hedren) pretends to be a pet shop clerk waiting on Mitch Brenner (Rod Taylor), who knows she is acting but poses as the unwitting customer anyway. As part of an elaborate ruse engineered in *Notorious* by a United States intelligence officer, reluctant agent Alicia Huberman (Ingrid Bergman) masquerades as a Nazi sympathizer so that she can ensnare Alex Sebastian (Claude Rains) in marriage and ferret information from the spy ring he is running out of his mansion in Rio de Janeiro.

Like Hitchcock's 1930 British film *Murder!*, the appropriately titled *Stage Fright* is rooted in the world of theatre and the backstage life of actors. Drama student Eve Gill (Jane Wyman) poses as a maid to famous London stage actress Charlotte Inwood (Marlene Dietrich) in order to get evidence that it was Charlotte and not Eve's friend Jonathan Cooper (Richard Todd) who killed Charlotte's husband. Everyone dissembles. Charlotte pretends to be grief stricken even though she was having an affair with Jonathan, Eve lies on various occasions to the police, Eve's father creates multiple scenarios to entrap the suspects and, most importantly of all, Cooper and Hitchcock (through a deceptive opening flashback) pretend that Cooper is innocent of the murder he turns out actually to have committed. Emphasizing its theatrical iconography, the film opens when a safety curtain rises to reveal a long shot of the city of London and ends when the police fatally drop the same iron safety curtain on Jonathan as he attempts to escape from the theatre where Charlotte has been performing.

North by Northwest itself opens like a stage performance, a feature which may be intentionally ironic for a film with such open-ended geographic sweep to it. As the intersecting graphic lines of the credits resolve into the frames and panels of a Madison Avenue office building, an elevator descends, the doors open as if they are the curtains of a stage and out strides Roger Thornhill like the big shot host of one of those drama anthologies so popular on 50s television. Thornhill is in total command of his surroundings, casually joking with the elevator starter and continually dictating messages on the run to his secretary Maggie. With notepad and sardonic comeback in hand, Maggie functions like a studio assistant keeping track of all the backstory alterations in the script that Thornhill believes he controls. Late for an appointment, Thornhill commandeers a cab from a waiting passenger by feigning an emergency. "I have a sick woman here. Would you mind terribly?" asks Thornhill as he elbows the bewildered would-be rider aside. "Poor man," comments Maggie, to which Thornhill replies, "Oh come, come, come! I made him a happy man. I made him feel like a good Samaritan." Unconvinced, Maggie answers, "He knew you were lying." But Thornhill reconciles everything within his special view of life: "Ah, Maggie, in the world of advertising there is no such thing as a lie. There is only the Expedient Exaggeration, you ought to know that."

This is who Thornhill is both professionally and personally. Smug and impatient, he manipulates the truth and chooses different masks to fit the occasion. He is incapable of empathy much less authentic love for another and treats everyone with the same casual disregard — the random cab-less New Yorker or the former girlfriend about to receive the brush-off note he is dictating to Maggie. Advertising is the perfect profession for Thornhill, who is reminiscent of Tashlin's Rock Hunter once he has become both successful and spoiled.

Randomness, however, can swing both ways. When Licht and Valerian mistake Thornhill for the non-existent George Kaplan and abduct him from the Plaza, Thornhill is indignant at being forcibly cast in someone else's production. His subsequent interrogation in the Townsend library is exactly that — a play meticulously crafted by, directed by and starring Phillip Vandamm. Just as Thornhill snatched a cab, Vandamm also has appropriated another person's property (Townsend's mansion in this case) for the staging of his drama. Adding to the similarities, Vandamm makes a theatrical entrance into the film much like Thornhill's; the library door opens and a well dressed, urbane Vandamm advances downstage toward the camera. Matching camera pans as Vandamm and Thornhill circle the room further suggest similarities between the two.

Most writers commenting on the library scene assume that Vandamm is specifically impersonating Lester Townsend. Certainly Thornhill thinks so; he notes the wrought iron sign reading "Townsend" on the front lawn as his abductors drive him through the mansion's gate, and he picks up a magazine in the library which is identified in the close-up insert as being addressed to "Mr. Lester Townsend, 109 Baywood, Glen Cove, N.Y." After Vandamm compliments him for having more polish than the others, Thornhill bitterly replies, "Oh, I'm so glad you're pleased, Mr. Townsend." Later, when his exit from the library is blocked by Valerian, Thornhill warns, "Townsend — you're making a serious mistake."

Nowhere during the conversation in the library, however, does Vandamm introduce himself as Townsend nor does any one of his assistants refer to him as Townsend. The Townsend pretense is specifically adopted the following morning when Thornhill returns to the mansion with his mother and the detectives. But what is important in the library performance is that Vandamm is clearly not representing himself but rather masquerading as an influential man of society (his "wife" announces that "the guests are here, dear") with proprietary knowledge of the house and a large staff of obedient lackeys.

In command of the setting, Vandamm moves through space like a director dressing his stage; he pulls the drapes of the library shut and turns on a desk lamp and then a light by the couch in order to better scrutinize Thornhill. Even though it is Vandamm who is concealing his real identity, he berates Thornhill for denying that he is George Kaplan. "Games? Must we?" asks Vandamm in exasperation as he pushes Thornhill for information. When Thornhill offers up his evening theatre tickets as proof of his normal ad man existence, Vandamm remarks that "with such expert playacting, you make this very room a theater."

Richly ironic is the fact that Vandamm is convinced that Thornhill is his nemesis George Kaplan whereas Thornhill believes Vandamm to be Lester Townsend of Glen Cove, New York. "So you see," says Vandamm, "there's very little sense in maintaining this fiction that you're deceiving us any more than we're deceiving you," yet that is exactly what they are doing. This interchange in the library is the most direct and forthcoming that Thornhill is going to be with Vandamm for the rest of the film, but Vandamm is too caught up in artifice to recognize the "truth."

Once past the central implausibility of the mistaken identity convention, the subsequent cross-purposed performances are easier for the viewer to accept. Following the library interrogation and the botched death by drunk driving attempt, Vandamm continues to dictate those performances. When Thornhill brings his mother, his lawyer and the detectives back to the Townsend mansion to prove his innocence, the Glen Cove play enters its second act. An absent Vandamm has cast his sister as Mrs. Townsend, Valerian as the gardener and Valerian's wife as the housekeeper. The story line is that Thornhill attended a party the previous evening as Roger Thornhill not George Kaplan, got himself drunk and drove away in a neighbor's car. "Roger! Dear! We were so worried about you," says "Mrs. Townsend" as soon as she greets the visitors. "Did you get home all right?" Playing to the authorities, she embraces Roger warmly, solicitously asks, "You haven't gotten into trouble, Roger?" and suggests that he borrowed "Laura's Mercedes" to "go home to sleep it off." Exasperated at her ability to sound convincing and framed by the camera in isolation from the others, Thornhill can only mutter, "What a performance!"

In his confrontation with Mrs. Townsend, Thornhill tells her to "stop calling me Roger," and soon after he intentionally adopts the Kaplan persona in order to pursue the abandoned investigation on his own. He impersonates Kaplan for the hotel maid and for the valet and gives his name as "George Kaplan" to the United Nations receptionist. Using his playacting skills here in the service of survival rather than convenience marks a kind of progress in the ethical development of Roger Thornhill.

The Twentieth-Century Limited episode offers up a wild confluence of overlapping playbooks. Thornhill is a fugitive attempting to be neither himself nor Kaplan and Eve Kendall is operating under the dual directives of Vandamm and the Professor. When Thornhill is seated at Eve Kendall's dining car table, he tries on a new mask and introduces himself as "Jack Phillips, western sales manager for Kingby Electronics." "No, you're not," she stops him. "You're Roger Thornhill…of Madison Avenue, and you're wanted for murder…on every front page in America." Thornhill admits to that part of his identity, shares the Kaplan backstory (conveyed nondiegetically) and allows himself to be seduced and hidden from the plainclothes police officers who have boarded the train.

Eve Kendall is supposedly traveling for business and is posing as an "industrial designer," a wonderfully vague vocation in the nascent tech world of the late fifties. She lies smoothly to the steward and to the porter and covers for Thornhill with the policemen by insisting that "he didn't tell me anything. All we did was chat about different kinds of food." Eve's charade may be the most challenging of all. As the Professor's double agent, she pretends to love Vandamm in order to spy on him and as Vandamm's mistress she pretends to have no feelings for Thornhill as she keeps him under surveillance (a facade increasingly hard for her to maintain after the romantic overnight on the Twentieth-Century). When the train arrives in Chicago, Eve joins Thornhill in performing an escape from the gathered authorities — Thornhill in uniformed disguise as a redcap and Eve as the random passenger whose luggage he is carrying down the platform.

The role of the Professor in these playlets is another important point of contrast to Thornhill. The Professor is the quintessential organization man. Games and playacting are what he does; they are among the tools he uses as a high ranking U.S. intelligence officer. He has neither compassion nor empathy for the marionettes he manipulates. Marian Keane has perceptively likened the discussion around the table at the United States Intelligence Agency Office to a "scriptwriting meeting" (p. 212). In the company of several other agents, the Professor reviews the various plot points that have gotten Thornhill mistaken for Kaplan and falsely accused of Townsend's murder and concludes that the play must be left to run its course. "We didn't invent our non-existent man," he argues, "and give him the name of Kaplan, and establish elaborate behavior patterns for him, and move his prop belongings in and out of hotel rooms for our own private amusement. We created George Kaplan and labored successfully to convince Vandamm that this was our own agent, hot on his trail, for a desperately important reason." If Thornhill has to be sacrificed in order to trap Vandamm, so be it. "Well that's his problem," concludes the Professor. For the Professor, the master script in defense of national security is more important than real action in the defense of a deserving individual. Additionally, the Professor prefers to plan or observe overt action rather than to participate in it. When something major goes down, he quickly exits the scene to plot his next move and to maintain cover.

Vandamm is similar to the Professor in several significant ways. He has authored many of the performances (the library scene, Eve's seduction of Thornhill on the train), but he avoids the dirtier work himself. "A pleasant journey, sir," he tells Thornhill as he leaves the library and instructs his men to "give Mr. Kaplan a drink." It is Leonard who forces the bourbon into Thornhill, and it is Leonard who receives the note from Eve on the train and who speaks with Eve in the La Salle Street Station phone booths to arrange Thornhill's bus trip to Prairie Stop. Most importantly, Vandamm also cannot clearly see beyond the playacting and the ruses to express genuine feeling or to accurately perceive trust (he learns too late, for example, that it is Leonard and not Eve who truly loves him).

After Thornhill survives the Vandamm-arranged Prairie Stop cropdusting attack, he shows up at Eve's room in the Ambassador East Hotel, pretends not to know that she set him up and makes no mention of the attempt on his life. Similarly, Eve pretends to have no connection to the intrigue and goes through the motions of rejecting Thornhill. Vandamm's earlier comment about the transparency of concealed aims actually applies here. Eve is deceiving Thornhill no more than he is deceiving her.

By the time Thornhill follows Eve to the art gallery auction, all the major players have gathered together for the first time on one stage. Vandamm as art connoisseur, Leonard as personal secretary, Eve as femme fatale, the Professor as disinterested auction observer and Thornhill momentarily between parts. When Thornhill begins to berate Eve for using and betraying him, Vandamm interrupts by asking, "Has anyone ever told you that you overplay your various parts rather severely, Mr. Kaplan?" Detailing the theatricality of Thornhill's behavior, he notes, "First you're the outraged Madison Avenue man who claims he's been mistaken for someone else. Then you play the fugitive from justice, supposedly trying to clear his name of a crime he knows he didn't commit. Now you play the peevish lover... stung by jealousy and betrayal." As if to summarize a capsule review of Thornhill's performance, he adds, "Seems to me you fellows could stand a little less training from the FBI and a little more from the Actors Studio." Different from both the Professor and Vandamm, Thornhill tries to anchor the spy games in their real life consequences. "Apparently the

Thornhill's impersonation of a disruptive auction guest secures his rescue from Vandamm's thugs.

only performance that will satisfy you," he says, "is when I play dead." Unflappable and still prompted by theatrical imagery, Vandamm answers, "Your very next role. You'll be quite convincing, I assure you."

Up to this point, the major characters have been performing mostly for each other. With the need to pull off an escape from Leonard, Valerian and Licht, Thornhill takes his acting public and transitions from chamber drama to sideshow. Pretending to be a boorish intruder, he shouts out inappropriate bids, starts a fight and gets himself arrested by the police. After he loudly questions an item's authenticity, a society matron sneers, "Well, one thing we know. You're no fake. You're a genuine idiot." Acknowledging the success of his performance, Thornhill simply says "Thank you" and continues the spectacle that affects his exit.

Because Thornhill's jealous outburst has caused Vandamm to doubt Eve's loyalty, the Professor is forced finally to intervene and admit to Thornhill the Kaplan deception and the fact that Eve is a double agent. Their conversation, played out on the tarmac of the Northwest Orient Airlines departure gate, is a key moment in the film, a turning point in Thornhill's development as a moral free agent capable of sincerely loving and caring for another person. When the Professor tells Thornhill that he has put Eve's life in danger and that he can save her only by continuing to play the part of the non-existent Kaplan, the camera moves in on Thornhill for emphasis and frames him in close-up. Shooting directions in the original script elaborate on the dramatic importance of this scene: "Turning to camera, eyes filled with emotion as he shakes his head slowly, trying to throw off the pain of his confused feelings...during this, another plane has been arriving, its landing lights slowly increasing the illumination of Thornhill's stricken face and the background behind him. The sound of the engines rises, as though illustrating the mounting determination within Thornhill, and his ultimate decision" (Lehman, p. 105). Accentuated by camera angle, lighting and sound, this decision becomes the redemptive commitment to a love that binds together Thornhill's fragmented self. In acting to save Eve, he further legitimates his talent for trickery and masquerade.

Thornhill agrees to perform in the fake murder the Professor has scripted for Eve to commit. In full view of a Mount Rushmore cafeteria crowded with tourists, Eve pumps two blank bullets into Thornhill in an effort to convince Vandamm that she has no romantic feelings for Thornhill and to generate a reason for Vandamm to take Eve along when he flees the country with his microfilm. Meeting post-mortem in the Black Hills forest, Eve compliments Thornhill's acting when she says, "You did it rather well, I thought." In agreement, Thornhill replies, "Yes! I thought I was quite graceful."

Cary Grant's grace, the echoes of his earlier incarnation as tumbler and dancer Archie Leach and, most especially, the film's inclusion of diegetic audiences watching Thornhill perform combine to transform our reading of the theatre motif into a reflection on Cary Grant as actor and Hollywood star. References to Grant's looks ("It's a nice face," Eve tells him on the train) are mixed with examples of Thornhill's effect on women ("Stop!" a female patient ardently calls to Thornhill as he tiptoes across her hospital room while fleeing the Professor). Additionally, Hitchcock elicits the whole catalogue of trademark Cary Grant mannerisms: the slow burn (as the elevator passengers mock him), the double take (drunkenly peering over the side of the Mercedes as it teeters on a cliff) and the comically grimaced mutter he perfected way back in *Gunga Din* (several interchanges with his mother). In crystallizing the essential Cary Grant screen persona, *North by Northwest* gives us Grant in the role we most remember and prefer — slightly devious urban sophisticate who redeems himself by film's end. Following the late 50s missteps of *The Pride and the Passion* (historical costume epic) and *Houseboat* (single father comedy), it is a role he would successfully return to in the 60s with both romantic comedy (*That Touch of Mink*) and ersatz Hitchcock thriller (*Charade*).

Thornhill's full redemption in *North by Northwest* comes after he learns the Professor has lied to him about Eve being able to walk away from the "dirty business" of counterespionage. The deceptive intrigue demanded of national security is all that matters to the Professor, whose callous disregard for Eve is opposed by Thornhill's fully realized love and compassion. Declaring, "I don't like the games you play, Professor," Thornhill breaks from the role-playing and responds with direct action. He escapes the hospital where the Professor has had him detained, climbs into Vandamm's cantilevered mountain house to warn Eve that Leonard has discovered the blank bullets and then famously crawls across the Mount Rushmore Presidential heads with Eve to evade Vandamm's henchmen.

The Roger Thornhill who risks his life on the side of a cliff to save Eve is far different from the Roger Thornhill who just days before scammed a guy out of a cab and worried about missing opening curtain at the Winter Garden Theatre. This Thornhill has resolved the alienated randomness of his life through commitment to another and has transcended the ego and possessiveness that characterize Vandamm's relationship with Eve. Just as significantly, the Eve Kendall who confessed earlier that "I guess I had nothing to do that weekend, so I…I decided to fall in love" has found new meaning in what was previously a meanderingly idle life.

The showy dissolve that takes Roger and Eve from Mount Rushmore ledge to honeymoon train berth affirms a positive future for the couple, marriage here, as in Shakespearean comedy, re-establishing a sense of order. There is symmetry in the Twentieth-Century Limited taking them back to New York and there is renewed sexual energy in Hitchcock's final smirky shot of their train speeding into a mountainside tunnel.

3: CLOCK WORK

Both Roger Thornhill and the viewer are continually aware of the passage of time in *North by Northwest*. As he races across the country trying to prove his innocence, Thornhill is pressured by a series of overlapping deadlines and schedules. Vandamm, Eve and the Professor also consistently check their watches and allude to time constraints. These temporal imperatives shape the narrative in significant structural ways by anticipating future actions, concealing plot implausibilities, regulating tension within a scene and even foregrounding the relationship between real time and screen time.

We first meet Roger Thornhill at the close of a business day rushing from his office building with crowds of New Yorkers whose lives are all tightly organized and scheduled. Dictating memos and calendaring future business appointments, Thornhill and his secretary Maggie hurry into a taxi because, as she tells him, "You're late and I'm tired." In the back of the cab Thornhill reads the evening paper and continues reviewing his schedule, which includes a 7 p.m. dinner with his mother at Twenty-One followed by the theater. The next morning, Maggie reminds him, "Bigelow at ten-thirty is your first…you're due at the Skin Glow rehearsal at noon, then lunch with Falcon and his wife." Cary Grant moves through his dialogue with the exact rapid-fire delivery he perfected as newspaper editor Walter Burns in Howard Hawks's *His Girl Friday*, and by the time the cab arrives at the Plaza, Hitchcock has established Hawks's same sense of breathlessness.

Between leaving Maggie in the taxi and entering the Plaza's Oak Room Bar, Thornhill checks his wristwatch three different times. "Sorry I was a little late" are the first words he says to Herman Weltner, who jokes that Thornhill will have to hurry to catch up with the drinking that has already begun. Once again Thornhill looks at his watch before explaining his need to send a telegram to his mother since Maggie won't be able to telephone her as instructed. The frantic, time-driven pace of the opening has intruded into the lounge's relaxed atmosphere and continues as Thornhill is hustled away by Vandamm's errand boys. "I left some friends back there in the Oak Bar. They're going to think I'm awfully rude," objects Thornhill in reference to the first of several time-specific commitments that will go unfulfilled over the next seventy-two hours.

An air of urgency prevails at the Townsend mansion as well. Vandamm has dinner guests and Thornhill has theater tickets, but neither has the necessary information to avoid a stand-off. "It's getting late," Vandamm says in exasperation before dispatching Thornhill on the drunk driving escapade. Despite his failure to learn about U.S. intelligence operations from the man he believes to be George Kaplan, Vandamm communicates specific locations and times regarding Kaplan's itinerary, information that will later guide Thornhill's decisions and that, in retrospect, will allow the viewer to accept the inevitability of Chicago and Mount Rushmore. Thornhill goes there because the stolen itinerary says that's where the nonexistent Kaplan is going. The implausibility of Vandamm possessing the schedule and the illogic of Kaplan ending his journey so near Vandamm's hideaway are veiled by the specificity of the information and the flair with which James Mason catalogues it.

Once he is arrested by the police, Thornhill's time is controlled by officialdom. Retained in jail overnight, he is forced to appear in court for an early morning arraignment and then directed by the judge to appear for final disposition at 7:30 the following evening. Another appointment that will not be kept, this appearance is scheduled for about the time that Thornhill will be getting himself re-arrested for drunk and disorderly conduct at the Shaw and Oppenheim Galleries in Chicago. Before being released, Thornhill is required to "immediately" accompany the county detectives back to the Townsend mansion to "determine if his story has any basis in fact." Although the visit and discussion of Thornhill's movements over time fail to corroborate his story, the phony Mrs. Townsend provides an additional marker that will become important in Thornhill's schedule — the fact that her husband will be speaking that afternoon at the United Nations General Assembly. Once again, Hitchcock is using time cues to lead us through the jumble of events.

As he will continue to do throughout his marathon, Thornhill remembers Vandamm's purloined itinerary (consistently the most accurate indicator of the film's movement through time) and shows up with his mother looking for George Kaplan at the Plaza Hotel. Time related details dominate the dialogue. Kaplan, the hotel operator tells him, "hasn't answered his telephone in two days." Upon questioning, Elsie the maid confirms that her first view of Kaplan (i.e., Thornhill) has been "out in the hall, a couple of minutes ago." Similarly, the valet explains that he picked up Kaplan's suit for pressing "last night around, uh...around six" although he only spoke with Kaplan on the phone and did not see him. Having trespassed into Kaplan's room, Mrs. Thornhill is nervous and anxious to leave. "I'll be late for the bridge club," she informs her son. When Thornhill answers a phone call from Valerian and learns that it was placed from the lobby, the resultant suspense is generated by two parallel yet competing arcs of time. Will Valerian and Licht arrive outside room 796 before Thornhill and his mother reach the elevator? The arcs intersect and all four characters end up packed (with several other hotel guests) into the same elevator car. Hitchcock structures the scene so that screen time and real time are concurrent even with his segmented staging that includes a dozen cuts, a tight pan and a backward tracking camera. Everyone endures the descent together, including the viewer, who is given the time to speculate on how Thornhill can make an escape. Pushing Vandamm's men to the rear, he helps "ladies first" and dashes across the lobby to the front entrance. Believing that a normal time frame still applies, Mrs. Thornhill calls after him, "Roger! Roger, will you be home for dinner?" (unbothered, it appears, at having been stood up for dinner at Twenty-One the previous evening).

The pressure of time conceals the irrationality of the United Nations murder that follows. After he tells Thornhill that he has been living in New York City for over a month, that his country home has been completely closed up and that his wife "has been dead for many years," Lester Townsend is knifed by Valerian and in the confusion Thornhill is mistaken as the murderer. Thornhill's panicked flight, the swelling chase theme and the abrupt end to the scene all work together to obscure the central question of why Townsend was murdered in the first place. He has no connection to the Professor, no knowledge of the Kaplan ruse and no incriminating information about Vandamm. He has already explained everything he knows about the masquerade taking place at his mansion. The function of his murder is solely to recalibrate time, start another countdown and initiate a relentless pursuit that will propel the rest of the film.

The first thing we hear at Grand Central Station is the off-screen public address announcer reporting, "Train number twenty-five, the Twentieth-Century Limited, due to leave at six p.m., for Chicago, will depart on track number..." Again, there is an alignment of Thornhill's causal and temporal goals: the need to evade the police and the need to meet a specific departure time. The station is appropriately frantic as Thornhill is caught up for a second consecutive day in a rush hour crowd. When Thornhill asks for a bedroom on the Twentieth-Century, the ticket agent looks at his watch and replies, "Leaving in five minutes." Impatient, Thornhill says, "Yes I know. Could you make it snappy?" The decision-making is concerned with time — no berths on the 6 p.m., the next train not until 10, the ever closer police. "You're in a hurry, huh?" asks the agent suspiciously as he tries unsuccessfully to stall Thornhill. Even the "meet-cute" with Eve Kendall revolves around time. Bumping into Eve while hiding aboard the train, Thornhill ducks into a compartment and Eve misdirects the police off the train just as it leaves the station. Eve continues to monitor Thornhill's time once she decides to stow him away inside her sleeping compartment. "Incidentally," she tells him after dinner, "I wouldn't order any dessert if I were you," referring to the plainclothes policemen who have boarded the train during an unscheduled stop. In the morning, as she sends him off to supposedly meet Kaplan, she is very specific about time details: "You're to take the Greyhound bus that leaves Chicago for Indianapolis at two and ask the driver to let you off at Prairie Stop, Highway Forty-One…it's about an hour and a half's drive from Chicago…he'll be there at three-thirty." In her rush to get Thornhill out of the station, she still remembers to ask, "Have you got your watch set for Central time?"

The Prairie Stop crop-dusting sequence is analyzed extensively in chapter eighteen, but I would like to emphasize here the role of time in its construction, especially the concepts of sequential order, duration and screen time versus real time. As mentioned above, the temporal framing is very precise. Thornhill arrives at 3:30 p.m., vehicles pass, a farmer appears and then departs on a local bus, a crop-duster attacks Thornhill and then crashes, Thornhill steals a farmer's truck and heads back to Chicago — the chain of events seems realistically to occur during the ten minutes or so of running time devoted to Prairie Stop. Verisimilitude is re-enforced by the logical, chronological order in which Thornhill's various actions are presented. He notices an image on the horizon, we watch him looking and we view the car or truck from his perspective. The local farmer directs Thornhill's attention to the crop-dusting plane and consequently we study its flight pattern. Shot duration appears to exactly match the amount of real time necessary for each of these events to occur. But within this apparent alignment, however, Hitchcock is actually both expanding and condensing real time. As the white convertible, the Cadillac sedan and the ten-wheel freight truck approach and pass Thornhill while he stands at the side of the road, the extended cross-cutting between Thornhill's expectant gaze, the moving vehicle and Thornhill's disappointed reaction when nobody stops occupies more screen time than would a single take with Thornhill and the passing vehicles photographed in the same compositional frame. Conversely, the amount of real time needed for the crop-dusting plane to dive, level out, bank, circle and make its various passes at Thornhill is reduced through a different use of cross-cutting. In this instance, Thornhill's reactions are intercut with long shots of the plane in non-continuous, foreshortened flight arcs. Both manipulations of time well serve Hitchcock's intentions regarding viewer perception. The expansion deepens our frustration that time is standing still for Thornhill there in the wilderness and that no real assistance is surfacing from the various false starts. Once a threat materializes, however, the ellipsis increases the tension and the feeling that events are moving too quickly for Thornhill to manage.

Hitchcock engages our awareness of time in another unique way during the crop-dusting attack. As Thornhill maintains his flimsy cover in the cornfield, he notices a tanker truck approaching from frame right. He also sees the plane banking for another strafing attack. Together, Thornhill and the viewer begin to make frantic calculations about distance, relative velocities and time. Can Thornhill cover the distance from the cornfield to the road before the plane passes overhead? Can the speeding truck decelerate before reaching Thornhill? Can the plane climb before colliding with the truck? Cross-cutting between Thornhill, truck and plane prolongs the questions in time before solving the equations with Thornhill's knockdown and a fiery plane crash.

Time continues to dominate Thornhill's thoughts when he returns to Chicago and shows up at the Ambassador East Hotel (remember, again, this is where the Vandamm itinerary indicated Kaplan would be). "Checked out at seven-ten this morning," the desk clerk tells him. It is this time specificity that reveals Eve's duplicity. "Well then, how come I got a message from him at nine…," asks Thornhill as he begins to understand how he has been set up. Thornhill's uneasy reunion with Eve in her hotel room is capped by two time-related agreements: Thornhill will have his suit sponged and pressed in twenty minutes and then will meet Eve for dinner. As we've come to expect, the dinner appointment is not kept and instead Thornhill follows Eve to the art gallery auction. With a continuously running commentary of bids by the auctioneer making us aware of the passing minutes, Thornhill tries to evade Vandamm's henchmen and "buy time" through disruptive bidding. When two Chicago policemen arrive to arrest him for the fight he has started, Thornhill asks, "What took you so long?"

The Professor intercepts Thornhill and the cops at the airport and brings with him a rekindled urgency that will be sustained through the concluding scenes. "Ah! Thought I'd never make it," he tells the policemen and then hurries Thornhill to the departure gate by explaining, "We haven't much time." In securing Thornhill's cooperation, the Professor refers to a deadline so critical that he describes it twice: the fact that Vandamm plans "to leave the country tomorrow night" and the consequent need for Thornhill "to go on being him [Kaplan] for the next twenty-four hours." Because he is trying to withhold information and conceal his real intentions, the Professor is always speeding Thornhill and Eve from one location or action to another before either has time to see the truth. "I do wish you'd walk faster, Mr. Thornhill; we'll miss the plane," he tells Thornhill in Chicago, and "Miss Kendall, you've got to get moving," he reminds Eve during the Black Hills reunion with Thornhill.

Believing the Professor's promise that after the deadline he will grant "blessings on you both," Thornhill meets with Vandamm at Mount Rushmore and pressures him on his scheduled departure: "Suppose I tell you I not only know the exact time you're leaving the country tonight, but the latitude and longitude of your rendezvous, and your ultimate destination." It is only after Thornhill goes through with the faked shooting engineered to lift suspension from Eve that the Professor admits he plans to renege and extend Eve's service beyond the deadline. "She's going off with Vandamm tonight on the plane," he informs Thornhill later in the afternoon. When he objects, Thornhill is knocked unconscious by a park ranger, and his "recovery" in the Rapid City hospital provides a time bridge into the evening.

A final recalculated countdown takes over at the hospital. "Inside of an hour she'll be gone," the Professor tells Thornhill in reference to Eve's departure with Vandamm. Setting and then breaking an agreement to have a drink with the Professor "in a few minutes," Thornhill escapes and rushes to Vandamm's hideout where he overhears that in "about ten minutes" the plane will be landing. Once again, Hitchcock puts multiple concurrent objectives in competitive motion against each other — Thornhill's need to inform Eve that her cover has been blown, Eve's need to avoid getting on the plane, Vandamm's desire to make a clean escape with Eve and the microfilm. The pressure of time is relentless. "He should have his wheels on the ground inside of three minutes,"

Leonard announces as he monitors the pilot's descent. Rather than crosscut between Eve walking to the plane and Thornhill held at gunpoint by the housekeeper, Hitchcock shows us Thornhill under duress and then concentrates solely on close-ups of Eve in motion accompanied by subjective tracking shots of the house receding and the landing field nearing. The tension comes from our awareness of the passage of time and the finality of the deadline. Thornhill (and Hitchcock) exaggerates the duration of this suspense when he rushes from the house accompanied by the sound of two gunshots and breathlessly tells Eve, "The housekeeper had me pinned down for five minutes before I realized it was that same silly gun of yours." In reality, it has only been about a minute of both real and screen time. The climatic chase across the Presidential faces, independent now of any imposed deadline, also plays out in a roughly equivalent alignment of screen time and real time.

Given the film's careful demarcation of the previous seventy-two hours and its detailed establishment of various timetables, the cut in which Thornhill's grasp on Eve at the Mount Rushmore ledge transitions into Thornhill's lift of Eve onto the top berth of the Twentieth-Century Limited sleeping compartment becomes especially significant. First, it is striking because there is no obvious explanation of how Thornhill is able to physically save Eve. Our last view of the couple is of Thornhill clinging to the cliff's edge with his left hand and grasping Eve with his right hand. The Professor and the troopers are far away on a distant part of the monument. Somehow Thornhill is able to hang on and find the strength to haul them both back to safety. More importantly for the discussion here, however, is the fact that this cut takes place outside of time. "Come along, Mrs. Thornhill," Roger calls to Eve, indicating that they have been married. But how much time has passed? Certainly it would not have been possible to get a flight from Rapid City, a marriage license and a reservation on the Twentieth-Century that same evening. Yet since Thornhill is wearing the same clothes and has his fingers bandaged from where Leonard smashed them, we also assume that a minimal number of days has elapsed. There is no definitive answer, and that mystery coincides perfectly with the archetypal nature of Thornhill's physical feat. This frantic journey from New York to the interior has been a bit of a fantasy all along, and the "timelessness" of its ending is an appropriate fairy tale resolution.

4: VISUAL UNITY

During the Townsend library interrogation scene, Phillip Vandamm pauses to discuss dinner guests with a well-dressed woman of the house and then turns back to Thornhill. Hitchcock cuts to a bird's-eye overhead as Vandamm asks, "Now, shall we get down to business?" In a triangular three-shot consisting of Leonard at the apex and Thornhill and Vandamm at the left and right corners respectively, Vandamm demands to learn all that Thornhill (as Kaplan) knows of his "arrangements, and of course how you've come by this information." Acknowledging that he doesn't expect Thornhill to cooperate without a quid-pro-quo, Vandamm ominously remarks, "But the least I can do is afford you the opportunity of surviving the evening." As Vandamm speaks, Thornhill slowly walks out of the triangle and the camera pans with him, ultimately leaving Thornhill alone in the overhead shot. Two visual patterns are established simultaneously — height to suggest impending danger and framing to convey isolation.

Hitchcock returns to the menacing overhead shot throughout the film. After the Professor and his colleagues have discussed the impact of Thornhill's mistaken identity troubles on their own intelligence operation, the Professor decides that Thornhill will be served up to either Vandamm or the police. In a cut to another bird's eye overhead, Mrs. Finlay remarks, "Good-bye, Mr. Thornhill, wherever you are." When Thornhill picks up the telephone in Kaplan's Plaza Hotel room and hears Valerian's threatening voice on the other end, the camera tracks in and looks down on a close up of Thornhill at the moment Valerian says, "We are pleased to find you in."

The film's most extreme overhead occurs when Thornhill is implicated in Townsend's murder and flees the United Nations compound. In a carefully composed Shüfftan process shot, the camera seems to look down from the very top of the glass walled Secretariat building at the antlike figure of Thornhill running diagonally across an entrance walkway to a waiting cab. He appears totally overwhelmed by his surroundings, his circumstances and his impending doom.

Eve Kendall is also associated with the ominous overhead. The opening shot of the art gallery interior is a high-angle close-up of the back of Eve's blond head. She is seated in the audience reviewing the auction catalogue as an unseen man's (Vandamm's) forearm is angled into the left edge of

The ominous overhead camera position as Vandamm threatens Thornhill.

the frame, lightly squeezing the back of her neck. Our concern over the precariousness of Eve's position as a double agent is emphasized by our not being able to see Vandamm's facial expression and by the potential physical violence of his gesture. Then later, when in fact Vandamm discovers that Eve has betrayed him, Hitchcock calls deliberate attention to the foreboding overhead. By firing the blank bullets, Leonard demonstrates Eve's treachery and questions whether Vandamm is still planning to take her with him on the plane. "Of course I am. Like our friends, I, too, believe in neatness, Leonard," says Vandamm and then, as the camera cranes up and tilts down sharply on both men, Vandamm cryptically concludes, "This matter is best disposed of from a great height. Over water."

Hitchcock's camera movement always signals intentionality, and here it clarifies that the menace of the overhead lies in its evocation of the actual physical heights that will threaten Roger Thornhill and Eve Kendall. There are three separate sequences in which height generates an obstacle or danger. In order to escape his locked hospital room and find Eve, Thornhill must climb out onto a ledge running along the building and inch his way into the adjacent room. Next, upon arrival at Vandamm's house, he must scale not only a cantilevered steel beam supporting the structure but also a ragged stone facade which reaches up to Eve's second floor balcony. As a kind of preface to the climactic ordeal, this rock climbing leads to the final chase across the top of Mount Rushmore where both Thornhill and Eve slip, fall and dangle from the edges before they are rescued from their pursuers. And, of course, in keeping with the association of high altitude and danger, Roger's Prairie Stop ambush is in the form of a machine-gunning biplane that swoops down on him from a blank Midwestern sky.

Up until the moment when the local farmer appears at the Prairie Stop crossroads to catch his bus, more than twenty separate shots feature Thornhill alone in the dry, barren landscape. He seems lost against the horizon, a tiny stick figure indistinguishable from the fenceposts. As mentioned before, Hitchcock uses reframing to show Thornhill first grouped with other characters and then isolated within the shot — a transition mirroring Thornhill's loss of supportive allies or his realization that only he himself can influence events. Hitchcock effectively uses this visual strategy early in the film to prepare the audience for Thornhill's difficulty in getting anyone to believe his innocence. The morning after his drunk driving arrest, Thornhill returns to the Townsend mansion with his lawyer, his mother, Captain Junket and Lieutenant Harding in order to prove his story of the abduction, forced drinking and runaway Mercedes. Failing to find the bourbon stains on the sofa or the bookcase liquor cabinet, Thornhill is then warmly greeted by "Mrs. Townsend," who treats him as an old friend and falsely but convincingly explains that Thornhill showed up tipsy to her party and left early. In the master shot all six characters are standing together downstage from the fireplace. Roger and "Mrs. Townsend" are on the left side of the frame and the other four visitors are on the right. As "Mrs. Townsend" spins her tale, Thornhill paces upstage and back growing increasingly angry and frustrated. When she asserts that he arrived by cab as an invited guest, Thornhill walks away from the others, and the camera pans with him, reframing him in a medium shot as he turns, stands alone and snaps, "She's lying." From this point on, Thornhill remains visually separate from the others. Cross cuts between Thornhill in mediums or medium close-ups and Captain Junket and "Mrs. Townsend" emphasize the fact that Thornhill's version of events is in direct conflict with the version that Junket is supposedly unraveling. By the time "Mrs. Townsend" reveals that her husband is presently speaking at the United Nations, a cut between Roger reacting to the news and all of the other visitors looking screen left at Roger in embarrassed disapproval emphasize just how thoroughly Roger has become alienated from friends and authorities. When the whole group leaves the library and then the house, Thornhill either lags behind to make a point or pushes ahead in disgust, the camera panning with or away from him to show his spatial distance from the others. Thornhill's isolation, of course, will reach its apex after he exits the bus at Prairie Stop and finds himself completely alone in a vast wilderness.

Camera pans in *North by Northwest* are also used repeatedly to link a character with a threat lurking outside of the frame. Once the roller-coaster narrative begins, Roger Thornhill is subjected to a string of escalating assaults and frustrations. Every situation he encounters is fraught with off-screen danger, and Hitchcock's restlessly probing and reframing camera movement keeps us appropriately unsettled. In the Oak Room Bar, early in the film, Thornhill snaps his fingers to summon the bellboy so that he can send a telegram to his mother. At the moment Thornhill calls "boy," the camera pans to the right, zooming from a long shot to a low angle medium close-up of Licht and Valerian, who now mistakenly believe that Thornhill is responding to the bellboy's paging of George Kaplan. All of Thornhill's subsequent ordeals emanate from this moment, which is strongly emphasized through the reframing. When Thornhill, his lawyer, his mother and the detectives drive away from the Townsend mansion after Thornhill fails to convince anyone of his story's accuracy, the camera pans left from the departing car for about 90 degrees and comes to rest on a medium shot of a gardener trimming a hedge, bent over and with his back to the camera. In a close-up, he rises from below the frame, straightens up and turns to look at the moving police car. It is Valerian. We are reminded pointedly that Thornhill is still under surveillance by Vandamm's thugs and still in serious danger.

Valerian breaches the frame in a similarly sinister way during the United Nations receptionist scene. Following Thornhill's request that the receptionist page Lester Townsend, the camera pans to the right, moving with Thornhill as he gazes about the room. It pauses at the entry to the lobby, where Valerian arrives and stands in the entranceway. The camera tracks forward as Valerian slowly slips on a pair of gloves. Soon afterwards, during Thornhill's attempt to tell the real Lester Townsend about the charade happening at his house, Townsend collapses into Thornhill's arms with a knife protruding from his back. As he often does throughout his films, Hitchcock breaks the action's full sequential chain here. He shows us the preparation (Valerian applying the fingerprint-concealing gloves) and the result (Townsend's death) but not the causal trigger itself (Valerian throwing the knife). Hitchcock is forgoing the fleeting thrill of a flipped knife for the lingering dread of the potential violence that waits just outside the frame where neither we nor Thornhill can see it until too late to avert the consequences.

Another way in which Hitchcock manipulates the causal chain is to plant a seemingly unimportant detail within a shot that will become significant later in the sequence. For example, when the car which is kidnapping Thornhill pulls up in front of the Townsend mansion, parked in the upper right corner of the frame is a white Mercedes convertible — the same car which later is sent careening down the winding sea cliff road with a forcibly inebriated Roger Thornhill at the wheel. Similarly, before the farmer arrives at Prairie Stop and comments on the crop duster and long before it turns lethal, we have already seen the plane flying inconspicuously in the far right background as Cary Grant stands at the crossroads and watches three different vehicles pass by. People as well as objects are also introduced on the periphery prior to commanding attention in the center of the frame. Arriving at the Oak Room Bar, Thornhill tells Herman Weltner and the out-of-town clients about needing to contact his mother. In a medium shot from over Thornhill's shoulder, the three men listen intently, and in the extreme right background we can just make out Licht and Valerian standing by a shop window outside the bar and holding a private conversation. Soon after they will shove a gun into Thornhill's side and hustle him from the hotel. While Thornhill is confronting Vandamm at the art auction about Eve's duplicity, a dialogue crosscut to a medium close-up of Thornhill reveals the Professor behind Thornhill's right arm sitting in the audience and pretending to be just another patron. Later, he will intervene with the police officers who remove Thornhill from the art gallery and will pressure Thornhill into flying to Rapid City with him. (Hitchcock's careful attention to frame composition is curiously and comically missing in the Mount Rushmore cafeteria shooting scene, however. Just before Eve Kendall fires her blank shots at Thornhill, a little boy in the center background puts his fingers into his ears — an unedited protective response born of multiple takes.)

In addition to frames that foretell, *North by Northwest* also contains frames that shock. The composition is entirely different yet equally effective. Rather than conceal a detail within a densely packed frame,

Hitchcock also will fill the frame with a single magnified image, an application of the visual story-telling vocabulary he developed as a silent filmmaker in England. Thornhill opens the Townsend library door to escape his interrogation by Vandamm, and the entranceway space is suddenly filled with a tight close-up of Valerian blocking the exit. Thornhill is held down on the sofa by Licht and Valerian, and a close-up shows his alarmed eyes watching Leonard's hand fill an exceedingly tall tumbler with bourbon. Toward the end of the crop duster sequence, a tanker truck barrels down on Thornhill; the camera zooms in for an extreme close-up as he shields his frightened face with both hands and then falls backward. Leonard fires Eve's blank cartridges at Vandamm to prove her betrayal and Vandamm strikes him, the punch aimed directly at the camera. An earlier scene where Thornhill meets Eve in the Black Hills forest after the faked shooting at the Mount Rushmore cafeteria also uses the cinema fist device. Thornhill argues with the Professor over the plan to have Eve leave the country with Vandamm and tries to pull Eve from her car. A hand enters the frame from off-screen left and taps Thornhill on the shoulder. Then, in a close-up from Roger's point of view, the park ranger punches directly into the camera, sending Roger to the ground in the subsequent high angle medium shot. The effect in each case is to shock viewers with either a new twist to the plot or a new threat to Thornhill.

That Black Hills park ranger scene is also significant for how it incorporates two key structural elements of the set design — verticals and diagonals. The establishing shot reveals a glade canopied by several dozen tall evergreen trees. Slender bare trunks fill the frame and are particularly dense in the center foreground. Thrust in from the left and right corners and forming an inverted V-shape are the green forest service station wagon transporting Thornhill and the white Lincoln convertible that Eve is driving. Thornhill and Eve regard each other from the extreme edges of the frame, separated by the dense upright lines of the evergreens. As they do throughout the film, the verticals physically minimize the characters and anchor them into a stark landscape made formidable by the challenges and obstacles it contains. The diagonals of the slanted cars cut dramatically into what otherwise is a statically composed scene, bringing structural tension and increased awareness of potentially dangerous off-screen space. The diagonals, of course, also mirror the angled directionality of traveling north by northwest.

Other examples of imposing verticals are the skyscraper sides, the United Nations facade, the Prairie Stop fence posts, the Mount Rushmore cafeteria window frames and the sheer edges of the Mount Rushmore monument itself. Among the diagonal compositions are the walkway seen from the top of the U.N. Secretarial building, the train track cutaways outside the dining and sleeping car scenes, the endlessly receding highway lanes at Prairie Stop, Vandamm's Mount Rushmore house thrusting out over the cliff in an extreme long shot and the cantilevered beamed house foundation that Thornhill climbs in search of Eve.

The diagonally angled cars slice into the foregrounded pine tree verticals as Mount Rushmore looms in the upper right corner of the frame.

Saul Bass's credit sequence prepares us for the film's unique scenic design. Parallel diagonal lines enter the screen from the upper right corner, followed by a set of vertical lines appearing from above and below and intersecting with the diagonals to form a grid. Once the grid (which momentarily also resembles a mesh entrapment) is complete, the following titles scroll onto the screen and gather on the diagonals: "METRO-GOLDWIN MAYER PRESENTS CARY GRANT. EVA MARIE SAINT. JAMES MASON. IN ALFRED HITCHCOCK'S. NORTH BY NORTHWEST." The abstract surface dissolves into the glass facade of an office building viewed from a slight angle. The geometric lines become windows which reflect traffic traversing the street below. And the surface on which the grid first appears is tinted green, a color used throughout the film for cabs, buses, government vehicles and even the lighting in Thornhill's Rapid City hospital room.

Used more sparingly in *North by Northwest* than in most of his other films is Hitchcock's trademark subjective tracking camera. Two notable occurrences are Thornhill greeting the Prairie Stop farmer and Eve approaching the getaway plane with Vandamm. After observing the farmer's arrival in an old green car and staring at him from the opposite side of the highway, Thornhill slowly approaches. Two subjective shots tracking forward alternate with medium shots of Thornhill crossing the highway. Thornhill is uncertain whether or not this man might be Kaplan. The man wears a nondescript brown suit, displays no facial expression, does not return Thornhill's greeting and stares directly at the camera. The alternating subjective tracking shots allow the audience to feel Thornhill's sustained apprehension regarding this intrusion into what possibly is dangerous private space. Later in the film, Eve is being escorted to a private plane which has landed secretly at Vandamm's compound. Vandamm intends to dispose of her at some point during the flight, and she now knows it. As Eve, Vandamm, Valerian and Leonard walk toward the plane, Eve looks back at the house where Thornhill remains as her sole hope of rescue. The camera tracks backward from Eve's point of view and we see the possibility of Thornhill coming to her aid recede further into the distance.

Subjective tracking shots increase the audience's identification with a particular character. Rather than only share Thornhill's or Eve's experiences, we also observe, study and ultimately judge. Neither is a completely likeable character, and our allegiance must be hard won through approval of their actions and not bought easily by the shared frisson of a slow track into threatening space. Additionally, the narrative is moving too rapidly to slow down for the kind of sustained suspense that is built around alternating takes of a camera gradually edging forward (notice the lack in *North by Northwest* of any prolonged tracking scenes played out on a staircase). Among the many working titles for *North by Northwest* was *Breathless*, a choice which communicates the speed at which things happen to Thornhill. He is kept continually off balance by a world spun out of his control. What we share with him is surprise and what we come to admire is his resourcefulness in confronting those surprises.

The decision regarding subjective camera is reflective of the careful planning that characterizes the total visual design of *North by Northwest*. As much as with the spiral imagery in *Vertigo* or the confinement motif in *The Birds*, there is a unified visual pattern. Shot composition, camera pans and reframing reveal one unexpected landmine after another. With twelve car rides, a stolen truck, a train trip, a bus ride and a flight on Northwest Orient, Roger Thornhill is embarked on a single nonstop road trip. Hitchcock's mastery of technique controls our sightseeing gaze all along the way.

5: NORTH BY NOTORIOUS

Among the many fascinating aspects of Diego Velazquez's masterpiece *Las Meninas*, in addition to how it prefigures modern art in its multiple focal points, its attention to the space beyond the canvas and its self-reflexiveness, is the way in which it reworks structural concepts from his earlier paintings. There are the mirrored images of *The Rokeby Venus*, the scene-within-a-scene framing of *Christ in the House of Martha and Mary* and the confrontational gaze of the painted subject directed outward to the viewer that occurs in *Los Borrachos* and *Surrender of Breda*. Almost exactly three hundred years after Velazquez's 1656 original, Picasso completed a series of fifty-eight large scale oil paintings based on *Las Meninas* in which he experimented repeatedly with its treatment of color, light and composition.

Continuous self-reflection and reworking of ideas are what great artists do, and this running creative discourse with himself is evident throughout Hitchcock's career. Take, for example, the old McKittrick Hotel in *Vertigo*. A two-story wooden Victorian building, it stands back from the street and features tall narrow windows. Kim Novak as Madeleine Elster imagining herself to be Carlotta Valdes momentarily appears at one of those windows. James Stewart approaches the house with a combination of wary facial expression and subjective forward tracking camera. Inside there is a steep central staircase rising from a dark entrance foyer. There is potential here for prolonged suspense, but Hitchcock is after mystery instead and so he moves Stewart briskly up the stairs to discover that Madeleine has disappeared inexplicably from her second floor room. Three years later, when shooting *Psycho*, Hitchcock remembers the McKittrick and uses it as inspiration for the Bates house. Another female figure at the window and another steep central staircase inside a California Gothic. This time, however, suspense is the driver and as private investigator Milton Arbogast (Martin Balsam), slowly climbs the stairs, Hitchcock cuts in extended time between close-ups of Arbogast's expression and a subjective craning camera until the tension is finally broken by a high overhead shot which reveals a door slowly opening and the woman from the window rushing forward to slash the surprised and helpless face of Arbogast.

Hitchcock ranges similarly through his creative catalogue in *North by Northwest*. An innocent man on the run, Richard Hannay (Robert Donat) borrows a milkman's white coat and hat in *The 39 Steps* to evade two mysterious men who are pursuing him. Likewise, Roger Thornhill bribes a redcap baggage handler for his cap and uniform as a way of getting past the policemen who are waiting for him at the La Salle Street Station in Chicago. Once the police discover the ruse, they swarm into the station looking for Thornhill; a high angle extreme long shot shows them spinning around a whole series of redcaps and coming up short every time. Compare this with the overhead shot in *Foreign Correspondent* where a murderer disappears into a crowd of people holding identical umbrellas which conceal the faces and identities of everyone, including the murderer.

Toward the end of *The 39 Steps*, Hannay is cornered by police in the Palladium audience and disrupts a variety show in order to prove that the performer, Mr. Memory, is involved in the theft of secret documents. Roger Thornhill does something very similar in *North by Northwest* when he heckles the auctioneer and starts a fight at the Shaw and Oppenheim Galleries so that the police will be summoned and will hustle him out of reach of Vandamm's henchmen.

At 136 minutes, *North by Northwest* is Hitchcock's longest film; its length and geographical scope provide multiple opportunities for reflecting on previous work. A partial list of those references includes the following:

> The villain (Norman Lloyd) dangling from the side of the Statue of Liberty in *Saboteur* becomes Thornhill and Eve clinging to the steep edge of Mount Rushmore. Hitchcock later told Truffaut that having the hero and heroine in danger rather than the villain increased the audience's anguish and thereby improved the scene. *Saboteur's* hero Barry Kane (Robert Cummings) tries to pull Lloyd to safety, fails and is in turn clasped and hauled back onto the statue's railing by Priscilla Lane. In *North by Northwest*, Leonard tries to push Thornhill and Eve from the cliff and instead plunges to the rocks himself after being shot, allowing Thornhill to strengthen his grip and save Eve.

In both *The 39 Steps* and the second *The Man Who Knew Too Much*, a victim is stabbed in the back and falls into the arms of the main character, a predicament also faced by Thornhill in *North by Northwest*. Both Thornhill and James Stewart in *The Man Who Knew Too Much* remove the knife, placing each of them in further personal danger.

Trains are used as means of escape or as deceptively fortuitous meeting place in *The Lady Vanishes*, *The 39 Steps*, *Secret Agent*, *Suspicion*, *Shadow of a Doubt*, *Strangers on a Train* and, of course, *North by Northwest*.

The implausible turning of a windmill against the direction of the wind means trouble within for Johnny Jones (Joel McCrea) in *Foreign Correspondent*. A similarly ominous lapse in mechanical logic occurs in *North by Northwest* with the observation that an airplane is "dustin' crops where there ain't no crops."

A plane is signaled from the ground and lands to assist the villains in *Foreign Correspondent*. A plane is signaled from the ground and lands to help Vandamm flee the country in *North by Northwest*.

Photographs of Richard Hannay, Barry Kane and Roger Thornhill appear in newspaper stories that inaccurately implicate them in murders they did not commit. Those photographs are used by various people to identify and turn them into the authorities, including Pamela (Madeleine Carroll) twice in *The 39 Steps* and the Grand Central Station ticket agent in *North by Northwest*.

In *Strangers on a Train*, Bruno Anthony (Robert Walker) intends to use a personally engraved cigarette lighter belonging to Guy Haines (Farly Granger) to identify Guy and falsely place him at a murder scene. Roger Thornhill uses a personally monogrammed matchbook to identify himself to Eve Kendall as he hides on a balcony above her.

Vandamm's housekeeper Anna lies to the police about Thornhill's abduction and pulls a gun on Thornhill at Vandamm's Mount Rushmore hideaway. She joins a string of hostile and or meddlesome housekeepers/maids who make trouble for

Hitchcock's main characters — Mrs. Danvers in *Rebecca*, Milly in *Under Capricorn* and Nellie in *Stage Fright*.

Johnny Jones convinces the police to return with him in *Foreign Correspondent* to a windmill which previously harbored a getaway car, a kidnapping victim and a gang of villains. Upon arrival, the police find no evidence of Johnny's story. One of the gang members pretends to be a vagrant. When Roger Thornhill returns with the authorities to the Townsend mansion, all the physical evidence has been cleared up and "Mrs. Townsend" thoroughly denies Thornhill's version of the night before. One of Vandamm's thugs pretends to be the gardener.

At the art auction, Vandamm rests his hand at the base of Eve Kendall's neck, an ambiguous gesture which could easily transform into a strangle. Swan in *Dial M for Murder*, Uncle Charlie in *Shadow of a Doubt* and Bruno Anthony in *Strangers on a Train* all prefer strangulation as their means of assault.

The most sustained and elaborate correspondences in *North by Northwest*, however, are with *Notorious*. More than a referencing of the earlier work, *North by Northwest* is a total re-imagining of it, an opportunity for Hitchcock, Picasso to his own Velazquez, to take his mid-40s masterpiece and expose it to postwar issues of consumerism, urbanization, big government and emergent feminism. Like a modern musician, Hitchcock riffs on his original melodic line with new harmonic substitutions and with virtuoso crop-dusting solos.

Both *Notorious* and *North by Northwest* are centered around a love triangle: a beautiful female agent working undercover as the wife/mistress of a foreign spy yet truly in love with a hero either voluntarily or reluctantly connected with U.S. intelligence. Played in both instances by Cary Grant, the hero is handsome and jealous, the villain is charming and cultured and the woman is alluring and imperiled.

In *Notorious*, Alicia Huberman is a dissolute party girl with alcohol and relationship issues. The daughter of a Nazi agent convicted of treason, she drinks excessively and agrees to go on sailing trips with wealthy older suitors. Early on in both *Notorious* and *North by Northwest* there are drunk driving sequences, but the one in *Notorious* has Alicia not Cary Grant at the wheel, and the blurry subjective camera shots are all from her point of view. Cary Grant (Devlin) is present as a passenger and his firm, steady hands hover under hers, ready to take control of the wheel if necessary and quick to flash his official identification card at the cop who stops them. The idea of control is important because for most of the film Alicia is dominated and directed by men. As Laura Mulvey and others have noted, whoever controls the gaze in Hollywood cinema controls the narrative, and we continually see Alicia through the admiring glances of the dominant male characters — Devlin regarding her reflected profile in the plane window above Rio, Alex Sebastian glimpsing her on the horse trail, Sebastian's guests greeting her at his dinner party. Essentially passive, Alicia pursues her major actions (romancing, marrying and spying on Sebastian) upon the instructions of security head Paul Prescott (Louis Calhern). Alicia implores Devlin to tell her not to take the job of bedding down with Sebastian, but Devlin remains obstinately silent on the issue. After a burst of initiative in which she impinges on Sebastian's privacy and his secrets, she retreats back into a submissiveness compounded by the fact that Sebastian and his mother have discovered her betrayal and are slowly poisoning her. By the time Devlin storms the castle to waken his sleeping beauty, Alicia is almost comatose.

Eve Kendall is a far different character from the helpless Alicia. Even though she is first introduced to us by way of Thornhill's appreciative stare at her tightly sheathed backside retreating down the train corridor, Eve is a strong willed and independent woman. She aggressively seduces Thornhill on her own and even briefly turns the sexual objectification tables on him by telling him over dinner that he has a "nice face." She introduces herself as an industrial designer, which may or may not be a cover, and pulls it off convincingly while also deftly manipulating the police and railroad employees with her feints and falsehoods. Another major difference between Alicia and Eve is that Eve already has known and been in love with Phillip Vandamm before she learns of his true nature and agrees to spy on him for U.S. intelligence. She does not entrap him the way Alicia does with Sebastian. Once committed to the assignment, however, she pursues it with fierce dedication, sending Thornhill off to his presumed death at Prairie Stop so as not to arouse Vandamm's suspicions and even acceding to the Professor's order that she leave the country with Vandamm after she and Thornhill have reconciled and admitted their love for each other. She does all of this fully aware of the moral compromises required of her and of the real personal danger she faces. Once her cover is blown and Thornhill intervenes to save her, she has the presence of mind to grab the microfilm filled statuette before scrambling off across Mount Rushmore with Thornhill.

Cary Grant portrays vastly different characters in the two films, stretching the definition of "hero" in both but in dissimilar ways. Devlin is a flat character who remains bitter and distant from beginning to end. He resents the fact that Alicia is forced to sleep with another man but does little to stop it other than to blame her. He is a good soldier, a company man, who spends a lot of time sitting on a park bench conveying instructions to Alicia or receiving reports from her. For an agent in the field, he is involved in very little action, apart from the discovery of the uranium filled wine bottle at Sebastian's party and the final rescue of Alicia. It takes Alicia's near death to convince Devlin that maybe her orders weren't exactly her own fault.

Thornhill, on the other hand, never stops moving. Neither an agent nor a good soldier, he is simply trying to stay alive and clear his name. Smart-assed and cocky, he personifies the urbanization and commodification of America. As an advertising executive, he believes in the power of the Big Lie and has no trouble taking advantage of other people. Once his sense of security is stripped away, however, he relies on his street smarts to survive, reluctantly working with the Professor but certainly never a true believer in intelligence gathering as top priority. Unlike Devlin, he immediately objects to Eve's role under the covers and puts his jealousy to active use by intervening in various ways to rescue her.

Both *Notorious* and *North by Northwest* contain a highly erotic love scene featuring an extended circular kiss. In *Notorious* Devlin gives in to his feelings for Alicia on the balcony of her Rio apartment and as the camera tracks in a circle around them, embraces her in a kiss that continues from the balcony to the phone and to the door. Likewise, in *North by Northwest*, Thornhill and Eve embrace against the wall of Eve's train compartment, and as they kiss their bodies rotate over each other in two complete reversals of position. The blocking and camera work are equally complex in both cases even though Thornhill's unqualified passion for Eve seems slightly more convincing than Devlin's for Alicia.

If Alicia Huberman is helpless, Alex Sebastian is hapless. More a victim than victimizer, he probably loves Alicia more than Devlin does, allowing her to snare him in a marriage that violates his trust and exposes his secrets. A member rather than commander of the Rio spy ring, Alex is continually bullied by his mother and by putative leader Eric Mathis (Ivan Triesault). Not as tall as Alicia, he often appears overshadowed by her, a kind of vulnerability emphasized at the end of the film when he begs Devlin to take him along in the car that is rescuing Alicia only to be refused and forced to walk back into the mansion to confront a probable death sentence from Eric.

Phillip Vandamm takes orders from no one; he only gives orders. As wealthy and cultured as Sebastian, he uses his personal assistant Leonard and his hired guns Valerian and Licht to carry out the violence he prefers to directly avoid himself. Believing Thornhill to be a pursuing U.S. agent, he tries repeatedly to have him killed, each attempt more elaborate than the previous. Vandamm's interest in Eve Kendall is more proprietary than romantic — she is another beautiful trophy for his art collection. We watch Alex Sebastian tenderly holding or kissing Alicia's hand whereas we never see Vandamm caressing Eve only possessively clasping her by the back of the neck. No matter the situation, Vandamm maintains his debonair tranquility and, unlike Sebastian, remains unruffled even at the end when his operation is finally destroyed. Quick as always with a witty remark, he watches Leonard get shot from the side of Mount Rushmore by state troopers and deadpans, "That wasn't very sporting, using real bullets!"

In both films the lovers are kept apart by the demands of United States intelligence agencies. Devlin reports to a boss and an organization that are fairly loose and low-key. Agency chief Prescott is very informal with Devlin, giving him personal advice and chatting casually with him while eating crackers and cheese in bed. Alicia's willingness to work undercover is important to Prescott, but he does not pressure her to support the mission above all else. Prescott initially withholds some critical information from Devlin regarding the nature of Alicia's assignment and Devlin angrily accuses agency officials of hypocrisy when they refer to Alicia as "a woman of that sort" while their wives safely play bridge in Washington, but in general Prescott's intelligence operation comes off as a necessary function of national security.

By contrast, the Professor's organization is bureaucratic and ruthless, representative of the abuses of big government. Housed in a nondescript office within sight of the Capitol, the Professor and his associates sit around a conference table discussing people as if they were expendable chess pieces. Thornhill must be sacrificed and Eve Kendall must complete her assignment at any cost. The Professor's authority is absolute; with a wave of his ID he commands city police, federal rangers and state troopers. When Thornhill mutinies and sets out to rescue Eve on his own, he is also (by extension) resisting the unchecked power of subterfuge government.

In *Notorious* and *North by Northwest*, the pursuit of personal love trumps the pursuit of international politics. The message conveyed by both films is that love has the power to redeem the past and reclaim the best impulses of those who commit to it. Once Devlin and Alicia leave Miami, their story plays out entirely in a Rio comprised of studio sets, second unit footage and rear projections. *North by Northwest* moves from the east coast to the Midwest and back again, making extensive use of complicated location shooting. Both works reveal Hitchcock at his best. *Notorious* is an exquisite chamber piece, perfect in its simplicity and containment. *North by Northwest* is a wild jazz symphony, extravagant in both its tone and its range.

6: OTHER IDENTIFIED OBJECTS

Early on in *Paterson*, William Carlos Williams writes, "Say it, no ideas but in things" (p. 14). That affinity for the clarity and concreteness of objects is an aesthetic principle internalized by Hitchcock. Shaped by the structural imperative of his silent films to utilize cut-ins of objects to advance the story, Hitchcock also memorably foregrounds concrete signifiers in his sound films for emotional or thematic impact. Recall the key in *Notorious*, the glass of milk in *Suspicion*, the bloody doll in *Stage Fright*. In fact, just as he reworks plot points, Hitchcock returns throughout his career to a catalogue of recurrent objects that accrue meaning both for the individual film and for his work as a whole. *North by Northwest* riffs on several of the essential ones.

CIGARETTES. How you smoke a cigarette in a Hitchcock movie indicates what kind of person you are. Licht does it Gestapo-style, cigarette clutched between thumb and forefinger, like Major Strasser in *Casablanca*. Along with his scowl, the gesture connotes brutality just as Madame Sebastian's slant mouth smoking in bed suggests coarseness. Vandamm smokes with the same sophistication that defines his behavior throughout the film. Wordlessly directing Leonard to fetch his cigarette from a pocket case, Vandamm waits for it to be lighted and then holds the cigarette between the first two fingers of his right hand while fastidiously cupping the thumb and fingers of his left hand. Eve Kendall uses the lighting of her cigarette as a seduction ritual. After she caresses and almost kisses Thornhill's hand as he offers her a lighted match, Eve slowly exhales the smoke from her cigarette and poses it in midair like a chic accessory. Hitchcock apparently coached Eva Marie Saint quite carefully in the proper way for a beautiful woman to smoke a cigarette and her performance in the dining car is as stylish as Tippi Hedren's cross-legged, splayed finger cigarette break outside the Bodega Bay elementary school in *The Birds*. Roger Thornhill, interestingly enough given the pressure he experiences, doesn't smoke at all in *North by Northwest* even though his monogrammed matchbook, as mentioned in the previous chapter, is used for a key piece of plot related identity revelation in the same way Guy Haines's initialed lighter is used in *Strangers on a Train*.

JEWELRY. Hitchcock's guilty characters are sometimes given away by the jewels they display. The Carlotta Valdes ruby necklace that Judy Barton wears in *Vertigo* identifies her as Madeleine Elster just as the ring that Uncle Charlie keeps in *Shadow of a Doubt* implicates him as the "Merry Widow Murderer." In addition to signifying her social class, a woman's jewels frequently also are used to advance the plot, as when Tallulah Bankhead offers her bracelet as a fishing lure in *Lifeboat* or Grace Kelly baits suspected cat burglar Cary Grant with her mother's gems in *To Catch a Thief*. Eve Kendall's pendant necklace and choker contribute to her classic style, and her supposedly missing earrings give her an excuse to return upstairs at Vandamm's house to hear Thornhill tell her that the blank cartridge ruse has been discovered. As Eve walks to the getaway plane, she keeps looking back at the house for some sign of Thornhill's rescue, covering again by claiming that she's worried about the earrings.

MODES OF COMMUNICATION. Telegrams and telephones generally work against Roger Thornhill's best interests in *North by Northwest*. It is the desire to send a telegram in the Oak Room Bar that gets him mistaken for George Kaplan in the first place. By picking up the phone in Kaplan's hotel room, Thornhill convinces Valerian once again that he really is Kaplan. Much of Eve Kendall's initial duplicity in setting up Thornhill is arranged by phone. She and Leonard speak in the La Salle Street Station phone booths and she receives instructions to send Thornhill off to Prairie Stop where he will be attacked by the crop duster. Later, in her hotel room at the Ambassador East, she takes a phone call (probably from Vandamm) directing her to the art gallery auction. Thornhill himself makes two telephone calls, both to his mother, from the Glen Cove jail and from Grand Central Station. Each time, Clara Thornhill seems to mock her son and take his plight less than seriously.

With the obvious exception of *Lifeboat* and the historical films, it is difficult to recall more than a handful of Hitchcock films that do not include telephones or telegrams. Through telephone calls especially, plot information is communicated, characters are summoned, plots are hatched and occasionally, as in *Dial M for Murder*, individuals are directly victimized.

GLASSES. On Hitchcock's women, eyeglasses signify plainness and even shrewishness — see Laura Elliot as Miriam Haines in *Strangers on a Train* and to a lesser degree Hitchcock's own daughter Patricia as Caroline in *Psycho*. Sunglasses, like the ones worn by Grace Kelly in *To Catch a Thief*, suggest wealth, glamour and mystery. Hitchcock's male leads do not wear eyeglasses; instead spectacles reference the maturity and intelligence of older male characters like Sir Cedric Hardwicke in *Rope* and the Professor in *North by Northwest*. Vandamm's reading glasses, which he manipulates like a fashionable prop, similarly connote his cultured erudition. Male sunglasses conceal — whether it be the state trooper's motivation for stopping Marion Crane in *Psycho* or Thornhill's identity as he disguises himself in Grand Central Station. The breaking of those glasses when he curls up and hides inside Eve's locked sleeping berth is one more step in the progressive deterioration of Thornhill's formerly secure lifestyle.

CAMERAS. Shocking and intrusive, cameras tend to assault. Literally in *Foreign Correspondent* where the Van Meer double is shot dead by an assassin disguised as a photographer or figuratively in *Rear Window* where photojournalist Jeff Jeffries uses his telephoto lenses and binoculars to invade the private space of his apartment building neighbors. Roger Thornhill is compromised by a United Nations photograph capturing the moment when he pulls the knife from Townsend's back but which appears to show him committing the murder instead. Smeared across the newspapers, the photo is used by the ticket agent at Grand Central and by the Chicago cops to identify him as a wanted murderer. Here, as in *Vertigo*, Hitchcock underscores the dichotomy between the concreteness of an image and the truth of an image. The fact that advertising executive Roger Thornhill, who makes his living manipulating text and image to inveigle consumers, is undone by a picture ironically reinforces the camera's equivocal ontology. (Thornhill's television-age advertising sins also catch up with him when Valerian's wife pulls a gun on him after seeing his image reflected in a blank television screen as he sneaks across Vandamm's second floor balcony.)

However they originate, photographs linger in Hitchcock films like talismans. They suggest candidates for murdering a wife (*Dial M for Murder*), drive a villain to destroy every one in which he appears (*Shadow of a Doubt*) or remain completely mysterious like the never explained newspaper photograph of Vandamm displayed on the desk of Kaplan's Plaza Hotel room.

CONSTRAINTS. In *The 39 Steps*, unjustly accused Robert Donat flees across the English countryside handcuffed to a hostile and disbelieving Madeleine Carroll. *Saboteur's* Robert Cummings is also forced to prove his innocence while handcuffed and on the run from the police. Henry Fonda (*The Wrong Man*), Grace Kelly (*Dial M for Murder*) and Alida Valli (*The Paradine Case*) are all arrested and incarcerated. Roger Thornhill gets a taste of both predicaments. Vandamm's thugs restrain his arms to pour the bourbon into him and the police hold him by the arms as he is booked for drunk driving. He spends a night in the Glen Cove jail on this charge. On one level these indignities mark further decline for a once supremely assured prince of the city but on another level they also tease viewers with the hinted frisson of bondage and abuse.

AUTOMOBILES. Cars transport Hitchcock characters from one geographical space and one emotional state to another. The journeys are usually harrowing. In *Psycho* Marion Crane embarks on a road trip that takes her from spontaneous theft to brutal murder to ultimate swampy entombment in the trunk of the car itself. *Vertigo's* Scottie Ferguson follows Madeleine Elster in hypnotically circular car rides through San Francisco that lead to his obsession and her "doubled" death. When wealthy party girl Melanie Daniels drives her Aston-Martin from San Francisco to Bodega Bay, she invades Mitch Brenner's private domain and forfeits all her entitled defenses in a series of escalating bird attacks. Roger Thornhill is in and out of cabs, limousines, stolen vehicles, police cars, trucks and assorted government vehicles. *North by Northwest* is a non-stop journey that ranges from the Atlantic coast to beyond the Mississippi. Along the way, Thornhill loses his privilege and finds his character.

Some of cinema's greatest moments center on the sudden realization of an object's true meaning — for example, the blood dripping into *Rio Bravo's* glass of beer or, as previously mentioned, Scottie's recognition of the Carlotta Valdes necklace worn by Judy Barton. Part of Alfred Hitchcock's artistry as a visual storyteller, especially in such a heavily plot-driven film as *North by Northwest*, comes from this skill in arranging objects to emphasize their narrative impact, thematic significance and emotional resonance.

7: HANDS DOWN

In an article for *Hitchcock Annual* entitled "Hitchcock's Hands," Sabrina Barton suggests a uniquely revealing perspective for understanding the director's films. Key questions to ask while watching Hitchcock, she argues, are "Whose hands open and close doors? Whose hands have the agency and ability to affect rescues?" (p. 56). The answers resolve dialectical, gender-based issues related to control and lack of control, competence and incompetence. Controlled hands, framed by the camera as they complete significant tasks, denote power and agency. Involuntary, excessive or helpless hand movements indicate weakness or even hysteria. Almost always, the assertive hands are coded as masculine and the fidgeting ones as feminine or aberrant. That is why, observes Barton, "so many male murderers in Hitchcock's films are feminized or delicately wrapped in cinema's codified signs for male homosexuality" (p. 66).

Barton devotes only a brief paragraph to *North by Northwest* in her discussion but provides a starting point for further analysis. For example, Hitchcock's division of *North by Northwest's* "villain" into three separate individuals (Valerian, Leonard and Vandamm) can be seen in the way those characters use their hands. Valerian is brute force; in a typically revealing example, the camera tracks in on Valerian standing at the entrance to the United Nations lounge as he pulls a pair of black gloves onto his hands. In a medium shot later in the scene, he slides one of the gloved hands into his pocket and hides behind an archway. Seconds afterward, Lester Townsend collapses into Thornhill's arms with a knife in his back. Valerian's physical menace is made even more sinister by our seeing the detailed preparation for the violence rather than the simple act of throwing the knife itself. Leonard's hands are restless yet also responsive to Vandamm's needs and directives. He listlessly swings a croquet mallet, arranges his hair and flips through the sale catalogue at the Chicago gallery. As aide-de-camp, he also lights Vandamm's cigarette during the library scene and pulls him back from further involvement when Eve publicly confronts Thornhill in the Mount Rushmore cafeteria. In a most telling and dramatic close-up, Leonard's hands enter from the right of the frame to pour the tall glass of bourbon in front of Thornhill, who is being held down on either side by Licht and Valerian. Leonard's overeager sadism and dislike of Eve are communicated clearly as he sits in Vandamm's living room and a succession of medium shots show him pulling Eve's gun from his pocket, placing it carefully on a table behind him, approaching Vandamm with it hidden at his back and then brandishing it suddenly to shoot the incriminating blanks.

Vandamm provides the ruthless leadership that directs both Leonard and Valerian. He is intelligent and powerful. His hand gestures convey both elegance and control. Throughout his appropriation of the Townsend library, Vandamm is a picture of refinement. Among the cultured mannerisms on display there, he casually drapes a hand over the armrest of the sofa, lightly touches a forefinger to his temple, holds out a hand for a cigarette, places a hand gracefully across his knee, flourishes a pair of eyeglasses to read a paper containing Kaplan's itinerary and then dramatically removes and clasps those glasses in midair as Thornhill reacts. But there is also a steely possessiveness to Vandamm. The introductory close-up at the art auction reveals Vandamm's hand first caressing Eve's shoulder and then moving upward to clutch the back of her neck. Exiting his Black Hills hideaway to board the private plane, Vandamm grasps Eve's arm (and the statuette) in a similarly insistent way. Another close-up demonstrates Vandamm's coiled yet aggressive temper when he aims a fist directly at Leonard and into the camera after Leonard "shoots" him with the blanks that expose Eve's disloyalty. The infrequency of these violent, uncontrolled outbursts is reinforced by a subsequent medium close-up in which Vandamm winces and surveys his right hand. The symbiotic nature of Vandamm and Leonard's relationship is expressed in dialogue centered on body imagery. "Well, Leonard, how does one say good-bye to one's right arm?" asks Vandamm by way of parting. "In your case, sir, I'm afraid you're going to wish you had cut it off sooner," replies Leonard, knowing that his news about the cartridges will greatly disturb Vandamm.

As reflected in the power expressed through her hands, Eve Kendall transitions from a strong independent woman capable of influencing others to a helpless victim in need of rescue. On the Twentieth-Century Limited she is siren and seductress. Under orders from Vandamm, she puts the make on Roger Thornhill at dinner and invites him to spend the night in her sleeping compartment. During a series of close-ups, she holds her cigarette out over the table, glances toward Thornhill's matchbook, acknowledges the ignited match, pulls Thornhill's hand forward to light her cigarette and then, as Thornhill starts to withdraw his hand, pulls it toward her face again and slowly blows out the flame. Thornhill is understandably smitten. Eve continues for a while to control the events around her, revealing this agency through the work of her hands. She strokes Thornhill's neck in close-up, pulls a gun from her purse to fire the blanks that trick Vandamm and even grabs the statuette from Vandamm just before boarding the plane. But given Vandamm's menace and Thornhill's heroism, Eve is not to be permitted equal status indefinitely and, catalyzed by the extreme pressure of the Mount Rushmore chase, she morphs from femme fatale into distressed damsel.

She begins literally to unravel. First, she snags her wrap on a tree and Thornhill leaves it behind when releasing her, next she loses her heels and finally she abandons the jacket of her traveling ensemble altogether. Thornhill continually takes her hand and leads her forward. Various close-ups show her grabbing frantically at Thornhill's pocket and biting her knuckles in alarm. By the climax, Eve is dangling precariously at the edge of a cliff, saved from the abyss only by the strength of Thornhill's grip. Emphasized by a prolonged montage containing some carefully composed close-ups, Eve clasps the rocks with her fingertips, reaches up into the frame to find Thornhill's hand as it stretches downward, catches onto Thornhill just as she slips from the rocks and ultimately gets hauled to safety and magically up into a train berth as she and new husband Roger Thornhill return to New York. She has been rescued and tamed at the same time.

Thornhill's character arc tracks almost inversely to Eve's. At the beginning, he is unfocused and self-absorbed. "Initially," writes Barton, "Roger O. Thornhill lacks commitment, competence and control. His drinking and his divorces are coded as decidedly unheroic" (p. 65). His restlessness is communicated through his habit of continually thrusting his hands in and out of his trouser pockets. Most noticeably he does this during the library interrogation and while waiting at the Prairie Stop crossroads. As his mistaken identity adventure escalates, Thornhill's hands become busy with the tasks of intrigue. He pulls a knife from Townsend's back, caresses Eve's hair and neck in her sleeping compartment and punches an art gallery security man to affect his escape from Vandamm. Informed by the Professor of the danger Eve faces as an agent spying on Vandamm, Thornhill becomes the courageous rescuer, with a rush of determination and competence manifested in his hands.

He begins to wield a grip as superhumanly strong as Beowulf's. To free himself from his hospital room, he grabs onto the exterior brick wall and inches along a ledge until he is able to open a nearby window. Arriving at Vandamm's cliffside hideaway, he scales one of the support beams and clings to an outside balcony to observe Leonard and Vandamm. Once he learns that Eve is to be killed aboard the plane, he pulls himself up the ragged stone wall that extends to Eve's second floor bedroom. The physical discomfort that Thornhill has suffered throughout the film is concentrated now in his hands. A close-up indicates that he has scraped and bloodied his palm; he uses a monogrammed handkerchief to wipe the blood (just as the Professor pretended to do when he removed his hand from Thornhill's "wounded" body at the cafeteria). Pursued onto the top of Mount Rushmore, Thornhill pulls Eve through the obstacles, grasps the statuette, maneuvers among the rocks, holds back a knife attack and then heaves Valerian over the side of the cliff. As analyzed throughout these chapters in various contexts, Thornhill's final Herculean feat has him grasping Eve with one hand and clinging to a ledge with the other hand while Leonard slowly and sadistically steps on and crushes his fingers. Leonard is shot and Thornhill is somehow able to sustain that grip long enough to hoist Eve all the way up into their wedding night sleeping compartment berth. Moving back from a close-up, the camera shows Thornhill and Eve embracing. As Thornhill's arm circles Eve, we see bandages on his left fingers. The assault on his hands has caused no lasting damage; the transformation in his character is likely more permanent.

A close-up of Thornhill's hand conveys strength during punishment.

8: MYTH

A tall reluctant hero whose surname is "hill of thorns" and who exhibits superhuman strength scales a lofty stone edifice to rescue a beautiful yet flawed young woman named Eve. With these mixed references and more, the mythic overtones in *North by Northwest* seem as evident as the legendary nose on Lincoln's Mount Rushmore face.

North by Northwest's use of archetypal plot patterns has been established convincingly by various writers. First published in a 1976 issue of *Film Form* and later collected in his *Readings and Writings: Semiotic Counter Strategies*, Peter Wollen's essay "*North by Northwest*: A Morphological Analysis" demonstrates how Hitchcock's film follows the progression of narrative "functions" formulated by Vladimir Propp in *Morphology of the Folktale*. Dividing the story into some seventy interlocking segments, Wollen charts Thornhill's ordeal through sequential stages such as preparation, abstentation, interdiction, violation, actant villainy, dispatch, counteraction, downfall and rescue. Within these segments, the hero is given a task by a dispatcher who offers a reward (e.g., the dispatcher's princess daughter) in exchange for the quest's successful completion. The task involves returning an object of desire, which as usual has been taken by a villain. After a series of frustrations and hindrances (the tale's delaying mechanisms), the hero ultimately defeats the villain through combat, trickery and the assistance of a donor. Accordingly, hero Thornhill "claims" princess Eve from the dispatcher Professor after vanquishing villain Vandamm and securing the stolen government secrets concealed inside the pre-Columbian statuette. "The film, like the tale," concludes Wollen with the Thornhill-Eve dynamic in mind, "follows alternating rhythms of separation and unification, punishment and reward" (p. 33).

Similarly, in his book *The Hitchcock Romance*, Lesley Brill argues that *North by Northwest* operates as an archetypal romance as defined by Northrop Frye in *Anatomy of Criticism* — that is, a story whose plot "leads to adventure, with the killing of a hyperbolically evil figure the usual penultimate action and the winning of a mate the conclusion" (Brill, p. 6). By its very nature the romance is anti-realistic and artificial. "In the world of romance, whether in film or in other narrative media," claims Brill, "the ordinary constraints of natural law are loosened" (p. 6). Thus, the illogicality of its plot, the active role of coincidence in advancing action, the multiple references to fictionality and masquerade and its elaborate production values all reinforce the reading of *North by Northwest* as a romance. "The story line of *North by Northwest*," according to Brill, "illustrates the sort of outlandish adventures that often make up the plots of romantic narratives. It coils and recoils and exemplifies the exuberance of plot that characterizes many such stories. Like Sinbad the Sailor, Thornhill sails from adventure to adventure. In fact, a ship is practically the only common conveyance that he does not travel on" (p. 7).

As the *Arabian Nights* reference suggests, Brill pays special attention to the emblematic nature of the main characters. Thornhill is also a medieval knight questing for "identity and a proper mate" (p. 8) as well as Odysseus whose doggedness is rewarded "with a wife and a return home" (p. 12). Eve Kendall "retains hints of Persephone, the goddess of flowers and vegetative fertility kidnapped by the King of Hades and finally rescued through the agency of Demeter and Zeus" (p. 12-13). As twin embodiments of villainy, Vandamm is variously a "bandit and usurper" (p. 12) and "the devil" (p. 13) while Leonard is "an angel of death" (p. 9) and a "dragon" (p. 9). Taken together, the characters of *North by Northwest* act out an almost allegorical drama in which two isolated and incomplete individuals confront the evil of the underworld, eventually conquering all of its demons and redeeming each other through their tested yet resilient love.

A similarly strong case, I believe, can be made for how Roger Thornhill's travels mirror the hero's journey outlined by Joseph Campbell in *The Hero with a Thousand Faces*. In Campbell's paradigm, the hero's adventures can begin when "[a] blunder — apparently the merest chance — reveals an unsuspected world, and the individual is drawn into a relationship with forces that are not rightly understood" (p. 51). The hero may resist the call at first, but if he continues he will reach a threshold where he meets a shadow presence which he may conciliate, defeat or elude (the presence may also slay the hero and cause him to descend into the underworld). Once beyond the first threshold, "the hero journeys through a world of unfamiliar yet strangely intimate forces, some of which severely threaten him (tests), some of which give magical aid (helpers)" (p. 246). Among the trials may be encounters with a temptress and with a "self contradictory"

(p. 145) father figure who appears as both ogre and protector and who is not always to be trusted. At the lowest point in his ordeal, the hero undergoes a supreme test and gains his reward, which may be sexual union with the goddess/princess, atonement with the father figure, his own apotheosis and/or theft of the magical object he came to gain. The final movement of the journey is the return, where the hero "re-emerges from the kingdom of dread," (p. 246) and restores order to the common-day world with the boon he has claimed.

Applying this narrative formula to *North by Northwest*, the heroic journey begins when Vandamm's henchmen blunderingly mistake Roger Thornhill for their non-existent nemesis George Kaplan. Thornhill is abducted but continues to energetically resist his call to adventure. After he is forcibly administered a magic potion of bourbon, Thornhill eludes his drunk driving death and crosses the threshold into a dream landscape far removed from his everyday life. A series of trials and ordeals follows. He is confronted by the dark minions again at the Plaza Hotel, implicated in a murder he did not commit, pursued aboard the Twentieth-Century Limited, attacked by a machine-gunning crop duster and opposed by the dark forces for a second time at the Chicago art gallery. Along the way, Thornhill receives aid from his mother when she helps him break into Kaplan's hotel room and is tempted by Eve Kendall when she seduces him on the train and then sends him off to the crop dusting assaults at Prairie Stop. The adventure's father figure appears in the form of the Professor, who alternates between abandonment and assistance, duplicity and truth, in his relationship with Thornhill. After his symbolic death and resurrection, Thornhill confronts his final supreme test on Mount Rushmore where he defeats the henchmen, proposes marriage to Eve (who has been redeemed and functions now as the princess bride), reconciles with the father figure Professor (who directs the law enforcement officials in killing Leonard and apprehending Vandamm), secures the talismanic object containing the microfilm and realizes his heroic identity as a man capable of caring for and loving another human being. The film's final scene completes the journey as Thornhill returns to New York with his new wife and with order restored through the preservation of the government secrets.

In his famous book-length interview with Hitchcock, Francois Truffaut observes that many of Hitchcock's films evoke fairy tales (p. 94). Certainly the narrative archetypes discussed above suggest how *North by Northwest* works as a fairy tale but so also do the film's themes and images. Characters in fairy tales repeatedly search for answers to mysterious riddles, suffer betrayals from close allies, adopt disguises to survive and wrestle with issues of identity. Roger Thornhill is no different. Who is George Kaplan? Why have I been mistaken for him? These are the questions that consume Thornhill, send him racing across the country, expose him to multiple murder attempts. It is only late in the film, on the Chicago airport tarmac, that the Professor answers the first question for Thornhill by explaining that the non-existent Kaplan is only a manufactured decoy. But the second question is never answered fully for Thornhill. As in the case of Rosebud, only the audience gets the camera's omniscient viewpoint solution to that mystery with Hitchcock matter of factly showing the telegram confusion at the beginning rather than waiting like Welles for a tracking shot revelation at the end.

In his quest for answers, Thornhill is betrayed by three different people who present themselves as supporters. First, his mother fails to believe him in the courtroom and in both the revisited Townsend mansion and the Plaza Hotel scenes. Despite accompanying her son on his investigations, she believes that he is either imagining or fabricating the whole Kaplan story. Second, after seducing him on board the train to Chicago, Eve Kendall sends Thornhill off to the Kaplan rendezvous in Prairie Stop that she has apparently arranged with the full knowledge that an attempt on his life will be made there. Finally, the Professor double-crosses Thornhill when he promises that Eve will be free from all obligations after the faked shooting in the Mount Rushmore cafeteria even though he fully intends that she will accompany Vandamm on his flight from the country. The fact that Eve Kendall and the Professor both ultimately change back into Thornhill's allies is also consistent with the fortuitous reversals that occur in fairy tales.

Somewhat like a shape shifter, Thornhill takes on a variety of disguises to survive his ordeals. He presents himself as George Kaplan at the United Nations, bribes a redcap for his uniform at the La Salle Street Station, plays a disruptive drunk at the art auction and pretends to be a shrouded corpse after that symbolic Mount Rushmore cafeteria shooting. Each time he uses the masquerade to obtain information, affect an escape or confuse his enemies. Similarly, Eve Kendall disguises herself in the role of a double agent and the Professor passes himself off as a disinterested bystander at the art gallery and in the Mount Rushmore cafeteria.

Prompted by the disguises and his mistaken likeness to the imaginary Kaplan, Thornhill struggles with the issue of his true self identity. He moves through various stages of being. First, he is a self-centered businessman, then a fugitive from justice, a betrayed lover and then a deputized government agent. Finally, in true mythic fashion, like Wart becoming Arthur, he emerges as a hero intent on saving the princess.

The landscape through which Thornhill travels on his quest abounds with images from myth and folklore. The crossroads at Prairie Stop is the dry and barren wasteland which harbors Thornhill's most elaborate ordeal. Vandamm's mountain hideaway is the stone tower where the princess is imprisoned and awaiting rescue. In the cliffs of Mount Rushmore lies the abyss which threatens Thornhill and into which both Valerian and Leonard are dispatched to the underworld. The top of the monument itself is the sacred mountain where Thornhill realizes his true powers and secures the love of Eve. It is also the site of the journey's most magical act — the transfiguration or *deus ex machina* that somehow whisks Thornhill from the isolated ledge from which he is dangling by the fingers of one hand while clutching Eve with the other hand to the intimate safety of the sleeping compartment carrying the couple back to New York. In the world of fairy tales, the fantastic and the miraculous sometimes defy explanation.

Despite the use of formulaic narratives, the mythic conventions here do not confine or limit *North by Northwest*. Instead, along with the cultural references, the self reflexiveness and the stylistic exuberance, they open the film up and make it accessible and interesting to viewers on multiple levels. The archetypal alignment is just one additional example of *North by Northwest's* complexity and a possible model for critical appreciation of other Hitchcock films.

9: NEW YORK, NEW YORK

Many of Hitchcock's films are anchored in a specific urban milieu. *Psycho*, for example, opens with an extreme long shot of the Phoenix cityscape followed by cuts to closer shots which zero in on a nondescript building as the titles "Phoenix, Arizona," "Friday, December the 11th," "Two Forty-Three p.m." are successively superimposed on the images. Similarly, after the beginning montage credits of *The Birds*, a bell clangs, a cable car passes and an elegant, perfectly coiffed Melanie Daniels stands before Union Square, the San Francisco skyline framed behind her. *Notorious* opens on Miami (with an identifying timeline like *Psycho*), *The Paradine Case, Stage Fright* and *Frenzy* on London, *I Confess* on Quebec and both *Mr. and Mrs. Smith* and *Foreign Correspondent* on New York. In each instance, these opening shots, typical of classic Hollywood cinema, foreground a recognizable landmark or commercial sign to economically establish geographical verisimilitude and transition the viewer immediately into the narrative.

So too does *North by Northwest* begin with establishing shots of New York City. Not Brooklyn or Queens but Manhattan. Manhattan during rush hour. The abstract grid of the main titles transforms into the glass facade of a skyscraper where additional credits appear and which then dissolves to the entrance of a Manhattan office building. In a series of quickly edited shots, pedestrians traverse the sidewalk, employees exit the office building doors, a crowd descends to the subway, a city bus passes an intersection, commuters swarm down the steps of Grand Central Station, two women shoppers fight over a cab and another body to body knot of New Yorkers crosses another busy street. Finally, in a typically droll cameo, Hitchcock himself runs up to a corner to catch a bus, only to have the doors close in his face and the bus drive off without him.

This is the hectic New York City nightmare of every average middle American and onto this dynamic tableau sweeps Roger Thornhill.

Uniformed just a little more stylishly than his advertising executive colleagues, he emerges from his Madison Avenue office in full command of all the technological and human resources available. Dictating messages to his secretary Maggie as he walks through his estate like an aristocrat delivering instructions to courtiers, he buys a newspaper, weaves expertly through the crowd and commandeers a cab to take him and Maggie two blocks. Roger Thornhill knows every inch of Manhattan like a tour guide; within the span of just a couple minutes he mentions the Colony, Blum's, the Plaza Hotel, the Oak Room Bar and Twenty-One. He tells the cab driver to use the Fifty-Ninth Street entrance to the Plaza and not to "throw the flag." He is a prince of the city privileged by his gender and class to control the forces that surround him.

Hitchcock gives us Manhattan as Emerald City, the great shining metropolis celebrated in countless American movies — *On the Town, How to Marry a Millionaire, It Should Happen to You, Breakfast at Tiffany's, The Way We Were* and *My Favorite Year* to name a few decades-spanning examples. Just as in these films, the New York City of *North by Northwest* looks splendid. Arriving in New York by train as a new student at Columbia, Dan Wakefield in *New York in the Fifties*, remembers that "I woke to the bright winter sunlight reflecting on steel and glass skyscrapers packed in a proud upreaching outline" (p. 23). Robert Burks' crisp Technicolor cinematography delivers similar postcard perfect images. The sky is a deep cloudless blue, the cars and buses shine with newness, the streets are clean, the pedestrians are dressed in suits and dresses and the buildings, all hard-edged in the sharp afternoon light, are graffiti-free. Whether it be the rich wood and polished marble of the Plaza Hotel or the gleaming modernism of the newly completed (1952) United Nations Building, this bejeweled New York is far removed from the dark and claustrophobic docks that oppressed Eva Marie Saint five years earlier in *On the Waterfront*.

Roger Thornhill's self-assurance in navigating this Manhattan verges uncomfortably on self-importance. "I've never even been in Pittsburgh," he replies a little too dismissively to Vandamm when accused of having a contact there. Thornhill embodies the brashness that has always caused the rest of America to view New Yorkers with a combination of suspicion and resentment. It will take a forced journey to the Midwest to bring Thornhill down to a likeable size. Just as Joel McCrea starting out from the other coastal mecca in *Sullivan's Travels* will get schooled in the ways of the interior, Roger Thornhill will learn that material status is no match for the randomness and uncertainty of life.

As he flees the Lester Townsend murder he is mistakenly accused of committing in the General Assembly Building lobby, the process shot looking straight down from the top of the glass-walled Secretariat Building shows a tiny antlike Thornhill scurrying across the entrance sidewalk to a waiting taxi, an image which foreshadows the diminishment he will suffer west of the Hudson. On board the Twentieth-Century Limited without a ticket, he dodges the conductor and the police and wears a bribed redcap baggage handler's uniform to sneak off the train with Eve Kendall in Chicago. Like a vagrant, down on his luck, he shaves in a public restroom inside the La Salle Street Station and takes a bus with the locals to Prairie Stop, where he is again dwarfed by the endless open plains around him.

Thornhill's encounter at the Prairie Stop crossroads with a local resident is a wonderfully awkward moment where urban east meets rural Midwest. In a low angle two shot, Thornhill and the man stand staring at each other from opposite sides of the deserted highway, as mutually wary as beings from different planets. Determined to learn if the man knows anything about George Kaplan, Thornhill starts to cross the road, Hitchcock's famous subjective camera, usually reserved for intrusions into dangerous proprietary space, tracking forward to convey Thornhill's gaze as it closes in on the stranger's impassive face.

Their conversation is like something lost in translation. "Hot day" observes Thornhill, to which the man replies, "Seen worse." After an uncomfortable silence followed by information from the man that he is "waitin' for the bus, due any minute," Thornhill asks, "then…then your name isn't Kaplan?" Cryptically, the man replies, "Can't say it is, 'cause it ain't." In place of a good-bye, the man looks toward a distant crop duster and notes, "That's funny. That plane's dustin' crops where there ain't no crops."

On cue, the plane unleashes the most sustained punishment Thornhill will receive during his entire odyssey. He is buzzed, strafed by machine gun fire, dusted with noxious chemicals, chased into the path of an oil tank truck and then almost incinerated when the attacking plane crashes into the tanker. The once well-groomed, powerful New Yorker struggles back to Chicago in a soiled suit and a battered stolen truck.

Thornhill momentarily recoups in Eve Kendall's room at the Ambassador East, but as with Richard Hannay in *The 39 Steps*, another smartly tailored Hitchcock protagonist embarked on a desperate mission to clear himself of a false murder charge and to prevent state secrets from being stolen by spies, the ordeals will be continuous. Menaced by

Vandamm's thugs at the Chicago art auction, Thornhill heckles the auctioneer and stages a fight with security in order to get himself rescued and arrested by the police on a common drunk and disorderly charge, only to be whisked off by the Professor to Rapid City, South Dakota, where he takes those two blank bullets in the faked shooting and scales Vandamm's cliffside hideaway to rescue Eve. Clothed in off-the-rack pants and a loose fitting white dress shirt provided by the Professor, Thornhill ultimately finds himself dangling in a dark rural sky as far away from the bright lights of Manhattan as he could possibly be.

And so the education of Roger O. Thornhill is complete. The sense of comfort and security that surrounded him in Manhattan has been undermined and diminished. He has experienced the universe for the random and uncertain collision of forces that it is. He has survived his challenges not because of his big city privilege but because of his innate skills. Like Ulysses returning to Ithaca, Thornhill journeys back to New York, a wiser and somewhat more humble leader.

10: A DRINKING LIFE

Hollywood always has shaken and stirred its treatment of heavy drinking. As traditional a narrative device as car chases and dream sequences, alcohol consumption has been played for whimsy (*Harvey*), sophistication (*The Thin Man*), human frailty (*It's A Wonderful Life*), social problem (*Lost Weekend, Days of Wine and Roses*), melodrama (*Smash-Up: The Story of a Woman*), humor (*The Desk Set, Cat Ballou*), and even mystic tragedy (*Under the Volcano*). Cowboy heroes have been redeemed by kicking booze (*Rio Bravo*) and ice goddesses defrosted by sampling it (*Ninotchka*). One great comic (W.C. Fields) built a career around it, and one great director (John Ford) gave his Irish character actors enormous appetites for it.

In *North by Northwest*, Roger Thornhill's reputation as a serious drinker helps to define both his corporate lifestyle and his unique personality. During the opening moments of the film, Thornhill directs his secretary Maggie to have his mother meet him for dinner and to let her know "I'll have had two martinis at the Oak Bar, so she needn't bother to sniff my breath." When Maggie protests that "she doesn't do that," Thornhill answers, "Sure she does, like a bloodhound," a response suggesting that his drinking is regularly and perhaps justifiably monitored.

Thornhill is on a first name basis with the Oak Bar's captain and is well known among colleagues for the quantities he consumes. "I was just telling Larry and Fanning," says Thornhill's friend Herman Weltner by way of introduction to some out of town business associates, "you may be slow in starting, but there's nobody faster coming down the homestretch." Thornhill refers again to his cocktail lounge notoriety when he tells the Professor, "I've got…several bartenders dependent upon me." With the ease of a man who knows what he wants, he orders a Gibson from the waiter who seats him at Eve Kendall's dining car table, and he asks the Professor to bring a pint of bourbon to his Rapid City hospital room. "Better make it a quart," he adds when the Professor decides to join him.

Clearly Roger Thornhill drinks a lot. He drinks on business occasions and on social occasions. He drinks in the afternoon and in the evening. Carrying Eve's heavy luggage, he jokes, "I'm accustomed to having a load on, but what *have* you got in these bags?" He drinks so habitually and so substantially that when he is force fed a sizeable amount of liquor and poured into the runaway Mercedes no one, especially neither his mother nor his lawyer, argues to the judge that he could not possibly be guilty of a drunk driving charge all on his own.

In the pre-MADD era of *North by Northwest*, the seriousness of the drunk driving itself is minimized. The careening convertible with an incapacitated Roger Thornhill behind the wheel is intended to generate a sense of danger and suspense, like a thrilling carnival ride gone bad. There are blurred double vision point of view shots, close-ups of the car wheels teetering on the edge of a cliff that drops to the sea, near misses with several other cars and then the final chain reaction pile-up involving the police and another vehicle.

The aftermath is played for laughs. Held in custody at the Glen Cove police station, Thornhill becomes the drunk as noisy clown. "We'll get 'em," he mumbles to the night court policemen regarding his assailants, "We'll throw the book at 'em. Assault and kidnapping, Assault with a gun and a bourbon and a sports car." We hear his end of a bantering phone conversation with his mother in which he tells her he didn't get a chaser with all the bourbon and jokes in disbelief with her that the arresting sergeant is named "Emil Klinger." Thornhill's examination by the court doctor proceeds like a vaudeville routine:

> DOCTOR: Have you been drinking?
> THORNHILL: Doctor, I am gassed.
> DOCTOR: How much would you say that you drank?
> THORNHILL *(spreading out his arms):* Oh, about this much.
> DOCTOR: Mr. Thornhill, it is my opinion that you are definitely intoxicated…
> THORNHILL: No question. I'm stinking.

At the conclusion of this patter, Thornhill climbs onto the exam table and curls up to sleep.

The legal consequences are downplayed as well. Immediately the next morning, Thornhill and his mother and lawyer appear before a tolerant judge with the lawyer explaining the abduction tale and Thornhill's mother making humorous asides about the incredibility of it all. There is no mention of blood alcohol content nor property damages. Thornhill is released to follow up on his story with the detectives, and when Vandamm's associates sink his alibi with their perfect cover-up, Thornhill's mother dismisses what would be life-altering consequences to a contemporary audience by casually remarking, "Roger, pay the two dollars."

In his memoir *A Drinking Life*, Pete Hamill describes an alcohol steeped 50s New York environment much like the one Roger Thornhill inhabits:

> Home again in New York, after nine months away, I quickly fell into the earnest rhythms of the 1950s…Even in bars some things were not discussed. McCarthy was gone, but the Great Fear had left its mark. At the agency, I was on the fringe of the world of organization men, men in gray flannel suits, men who talked about the new cult of motivation research, of inner-directed and outer-directed human beings, of lonely crowds and hidden persuaders…I didn't want to accept those tame codes. But in an important way, I used them as a license. Drinking became the medium of my revolt against the era of Eisenhower…Much of my memory of those years is blurred, because drinking was now slicing holes in my consciousness. I never thought of myself as a drunk; I was, I thought, like many others — a drinker. I certainly didn't think I was an alcoholic. But I was already having trouble in the morning after remembering the details of the night before. It didn't seem to matter; everybody else was doing the same thing. (pp. 208-12)

Roger Thornhill drinks for similar reasons — to take the edge off his existential stress. Thornhill may be a master of the advertising universe but there is a void inside. Remember, as he tells Eve Kendall in the Twentieth-Century Limited dining car, the letter "O" in his initials "R.O.T" stands for "nothing." It is his fully committed love for Eve that fills the emptiness, the force that pulls both of them literally and metaphorically back from the abyss.

The final scene in the sleeping compartment is well detailed. When Thornhill pulls Eve up into the berth, we see that the fingers on his left hand are bandaged from where Leonard attempted to crush them. Nowhere, however, is there a celebratory bottle of champagne to be seen.

11: MUM

Mothers are generally problematic for Hitchcock. The usual narrative trope is for an unmarried male character to be fiercely supported by a widowed mother yet also emotionally manipulated by her. In return, the son is devoted and compliant but rebels on certain key issues like the choice of romantic partner.

One of the most intense examples of the pattern occurs in *Notorious* with the relationship between Alexander Sebastian and his mother (Leopoldin Konstantin), who is pointedly referred to only as Madame Sebastian. Alex and his mother collaborate closely as part of their Nazi spy ring until Alex falls in love with and marries Alicia Huberman. From then on, mother and son clash repeatedly until they discover Alicia's true identity as a US agent and reconcile over a plan to slowly poison her with arsenic. Even in the best of times, Madame Sebastian is cold and distant with her son but also aggressively protective, no more so than when Alex, like a little boy, confesses his marriage blunder to his mother, who reminds him how right she has been all along to be suspicious and then, while still in bed, scowlingly lights up a cigarette and begins to plot how they will eliminate this threat to themselves and to the operation.

A similar albeit less malevolent relationship occurs in *The Birds*, where Mitch Brenner works as a lawyer during the week in San Francisco and then returns each weekend to Bodega Bay to be with his mother Lydia (Jessica Tandy) and his much younger sister Cathy (Veronica Cartwright). Like Madame Sebastian, Lydia is afraid of being left alone yet also unable to provide any real warmth or affection for her son. She pushes away each would-be girlfriend he brings home and reacts with immediate dislike when glamorous socialite Melanie Daniels shows up in Bodega Bay with a pair of lovebirds for Cathy's birthday and an obvious interest in Mitch. It's only after Melanie is savagely attacked and rendered catatonic by a flock of birds at the Brenner house that Lydia lets her guard down and begins to show Melanie the slightest bit of protective comfort.

In *Strangers on a Train*, psychopathic Bruno Anthony (Robert Walker) is coddled by the emotionally unstable mother (Marion Lorne) that he would very much like to make a widow. And, most famously in *Psycho*, Norman Bates solicitously covers up for the widowed old lady who lives inside his head.

With *North by Northwest*, however, Hitchcock spins the mother-son dynamic for laughs. Reprising the comically outspoken mother she played to Grace Kelly in *To Catch a Thief*, Jesse Royce Landis takes on the part of Roger Thornhill's mother Clara. Rather than cling to her son Roger, Clara treats him with wry affection, always quick to point out when he's taking himself too seriously.

It is clear early on in the film that Clara Thornhill is an independent woman with a life of her own. Even though mother and son presumably share a residence (as Roger pushes Vandamm's men back into the elevator and dashes out the Fifty-ninth Street entrance to the Plaza, Clara calls after him, "Roger — will you be home for dinner?"), Clara has friends and interests beyond Roger. During drinks with Herman Weltner and the out-of-town clients, Roger explains that his mother is "playing bridge in the apartment of one of her cronies" and when Roger drags Clara along to the Plaza to hopefully confront Kaplan, she tells him, "You're ruining my whole day." Roger and Clara are more like contemporaries and pals than conventional mother and son, a relationship emphasized by the fact that actress Jessie Royce Landis was born the same year as Cary Grant. Continually tossing one-liners back and forth, they enjoy each other's company and on the day Roger is abducted from the Plaza's Oak Room Bar, they have plans for dinner at Twenty-One and then a show at the Winter Garden Theatre.

Clara makes her first entry in the film at Roger's courtroom appearance for the Glen Cove drunk driving arrest and immediately starts to undercut Roger's indignant rectitude. When the judge asks Roger's lawyer if he knows Roger to be a reasonable man, Clara rolls her eyes and sniffs audibly. Accompanying Roger and the detectives to the Townsend estate, she watches as Roger flings open the liquor cabinet and finds it filled with books. "I remember when it used to come in bottles," she deadpans. After every attempt at proving his innocence fails, Clara is the one who advises, "Roger...Pay the two dollars" (a reference to the Victor Moore-Edward Arnold sketch in M-G-M's *Ziegfeld Follies*, a film that Clara probably enjoyed back in the day).

Undeterred, Roger decides to break into George Kaplan's room at the Plaza to get some explanation of the mistaken identity and tells Clara, "Mother — I want you to go over to the desk, put on that sweet innocent look you do so well, and ask for the key to seven ninety-six." At first refusing, she falls in line after Roger raises his bribe to her from ten to fifty dollars. "Car theft, drunk driving, assaulting an officer, lying to a

Jessie Royce Landis, born the same year as Cary Grant, plays Thornhill's mother as sarcastic confidante.

judge, ...and now, house-breaking," she grumbles as they arrive at Room 796. "Not house-breaking, Mother. Hotel-breaking. There's a difference," Roger tells her. "Of five to ten years," she responds.

Resigned to playing a skeptical Nora to Roger's Nick Charles, she helps her son case the room. "Don't be nervous, Mother," he advises and she answers, "I'm not nervous. I'll be late for the bridge club." And this time he gets the last words: "Good. You'll lose less than usual." When a valet surprises them with a suit he's returning, Roger wonders why employees at the hotel have never actually seen Kaplan, and Clara says, "Maybe he has his suits mended by invisible weavers." Roger tries on the suit jacket to see how he compares in size to Kaplan and finds that the sleeves are several inches too short. "I don't think that one does anything for you," taunts Clara.

The most mis-directed attempt at comic relief provided by Clara comes when Roger and his mother find themselves wedged into the crowded elevator with Valerian and Licht. As Roger silently signals that these are the very men who assaulted him the previous evening, Clara leans toward them and asks, "You gentlemen aren't really trying to kill my son, are you?" To cover their guilt, Valerian and Licht start to chuckle and turn to the other passengers who look relieved and join in the increasingly loud laughter, a reaction which delights Clara and infuriates Roger. Inadvertently, however, Clara actually saves Roger with her inappropriateness since he uses the commotion and the crowd as distractions to elude the thugs and rush out the lobby entrance into a waiting cab.

In spite of her seeming disinterest and her wisecracks, Clara is the first person Roger turns to for help when his comfortable world begins to collapse. It is she who receives his call from jail and who shows up to bail him out. She is the accomplice who breaks into Kaplan's hotel room with him and she is the friend he calls from the phone booth in Grand Central Station just before leaving on the train to Chicago.

Clara Thornhill's most important function in the narrative is to make Roger likeable enough for the audience to care what happens to him. Roger is a good son. He supports his mother financially ("I've got a job, a secretary, a mother, two ex-wives, and several bartenders dependent upon me," he tells the Professor). He takes her out on the town and he banters with her in a way that suggests he can laugh at his own flaws. By stepping forward to help her son search for clues regarding Kaplan's identity, Clara signals to us that Roger O. Thornhill is worth saving. According to the archetype outlined by Joseph Campbell, she serves as a "protective figure" who provides the hero-adventurer with assistance in the first part of his journey. As he leaves New York and encounters Eve Kendall on the Twentieth-Century Limited, Thornhill passes smoothly from the care of one self-assured woman to another. Clara's quips and repartee have softened him up for Eve Kendall, who is exactly the kind of girl he can and ultimately does bring home to meet mother.

12: EVA/EVE

And so what to make of Eve Kendall? At first glance, riding the Twentieth-Century Limited to Chicago in her first class sleeping compartment, she appears to be one of the strongest female characters in any Hitchcock film. Like *Lifeboat's* Constance Porter, she is professionally successful and personally independent. A single career woman like Midge in *Vertigo*, she is also chic and glamorous. She moves through the privileged world of wealth with grace and assurance. In an early version of the script, Eve's profession was that of interior designer but since there was a real Eve Kendall in New York City working in that capacity, her career was changed to industrial designer. The switch is appropriate, giving her a more traditionally masculine sounding occupation. It is as a man's equal, in fact, that she conducts herself on the Twentieth-Century. She covers for Thornhill with the policemen, bribes the steward, steals a key from the porter and lies continually to the plainclothes detectives who board the train looking for Thornhill. It is significant that these initial impressions are dominated by examples of Eve's deception. Her strength, it seems, is treacherous.

Like we have seen with everyone else in *North by Northwest*, Eve is adept at role-playing. When she passes the "What do I do with him in the morning?" note to Vandamm, we assume that she has just been pretending to fall for Roger Thornhill. She lies to Thornhill about telephoning George Kaplan and after speaking instead with Leonard, she sends Thornhill to his near fatal ambush in Prairie Stop. When Thornhill shows up unharmed at her Ambassador East hotel room, Eve looks relieved but then immediately lies again and slips out to meet Vandamm at the auction. Seated there between both men, Eve remains enigmatic and hard to read. Thornhill sees only her surface loyalty to Vandamm, but the blocking (camera low and in front of Eve; Thornhill standing behind her) shows us that Thornhill's harsh words seem to actually wound her. Later, at the airport, the Professor tells Thornhill that Eve is an agent, and we realize she has been playing a dual role for Vandamm's benefit — pretending to be Vandamm's loyal mistress and pretending not to be in love with Thornhill. Even then, however, we are not certain of Eve's ultimate allegiances. At the Black Hills reunion, Thornhill pleads with her to abandon the plan to leave the country with Vandamm, but she tells him to "don't spoil everything now" and drives off in her convertible. Only when she is convinced that Vandamm is going to kill her on the plane does Eve disobey the Professor's orders.

Our inability to know Eve and Eve's inability to know herself early in the film are reflected in the way Hitchcock photographs her. Only intermittently do we see a direct frontal view of Eve. Her first appearance in the film is typical. She turns a corner into the train corridor, her head down and her eyes averted. In the "meet cute" near collision and comical stand-off with Thornhill, she is seen at an angle from over Thornhill's shoulder and with her face partly obscured. The reverse over the shoulder shots of Thornhill are positioned from the center of Eve's back in a way that emphasizes her perfectly coiffed blond hair. The first of many successive images foregrounding Eve's blondness, these "head shots" culminate in the scenes where Thornhill holds Eve's head in his hands as he kisses her and where Vandamm strokes the back of her neck. When she diverts the police off the train, Eve is seen in a medium profile shot and when she parts from Thornhill, she walks away down the corridor into a long shot with her back to the camera.

Both the profile and the rear views of Eve are repeated continually in her early scenes. The conversation about Thornhill's "R.O.T." monogram and the cigarette lighting seduction are filmed in profile as is the establishing shot of her reclining on the couch in her sleeping compartment. Eve is then again in profile as she stands against the wall of the compartment and embraces Thornhill. In the extended two-part kissing scene that follows (interrupted by Eve's profile-positioned conversation with the porter), Eve's face is partially masked by Thornhill's head and shoulders. Even when the camera tracks in for an extreme close-up of Eve's full face after she passionately kisses Thornhill while telling him he's "going to sleep on the floor," her eyes sweep past us and off into the screen right space where she has just handed the porter a note meant for Vandamm. It is impossible to decipher Eve's motivation or her true feelings here for Thornhill just as it is in the equally puzzling frontal expressions with which she watches Thornhill walk away from her at the La Salle Street Station and greets him when he appears unexpectedly at the Ambassador

East. Eva Marie Saint perfectly captures Eve's mystery as she shifts from amused detachment to conflicted involvement. Lowering her voice upon Hitchcock's direction from its normal register, she projects an assured seductiveness absent from her other screen roles and then, with a tensing of her body and a tightening of her delivery, she just as convincingly pulls back and seems to regret the whole charade she is performing.

The arrival in Chicago continues our inability to read Eve. During the platform questioning by the policemen, she is filmed from behind and in profile, and when she ends that conversation Hitchcock again gives us the full body take of Eve walking away from the camera and into long shot. In the backward tracking two shot where Thornhill carries her bags toward the main lobby, Eve and Thornhill discuss the details of contacting Kaplan and changing out of the borrowed redcap uniform. Not once, however, does Eve look either directly at Thornhill or at the camera. Instead, her eyes keep shifting from side to side, aware of Vandamm's presence on the periphery and concealing any facial cues to the emotion she is feeling. For the phone booth conversation with Leonard, Hitchcock starts with a profile of Eve from the side of the booth, cuts to a medium shot through the door of Eve looking off into frame right and speaking intently and then tracks laterally across the row of booths to show Leonard in the last booth presumably giving Eve her instructions. After the conversation, she exits and lingers in profile in front of the phone booths, glancing first toward Leonard and Vandamm in the background and then off-screen toward the men's room where Thornhill is changing. Her expression is intense, possibly troubled, perhaps masking regret or capitulation or determination. Ironically, she stands before the clear glass surfaces of the phone booths yet there is no similar unobscured window into her own thoughts and feelings. In a farewell scene played out against concrete pillars that tend to separate them visually, Eve is profiled in frame right looking left toward Thornhill. Her eyes avert direct contact with him, and an empty point of view shot reveals her to be deceiving Thornhill when she sends him off to catch the Greyhound on the pretext that policemen are approaching. Eve's final close-up is a rune, as devoid of recognizable markers as the featureless prairie landscape into which it very slowly dissolves.

During the Ambassador East and Shaw and Oppenheim gallery scenes, Eve struggles to control her true emotions in an effort that is emphasized by Hitchcock's blocking and camera placement. She responds to Thornhill materializing in her hotel room uninjured with a full clear smile of pleasure and relief and then, in profile, buries her face against his shoulder to cut off any further emotional display. In a tempered reprise of the sleeping compartment embrace, the camera tracks circularly right to the back of Eve's head, but this time Thornhill refuses to complete the caress and holds his arms suspended in midair (what to do with all that blondness?). Aware of Thornhill's mounting anger and suspicion, Eve turns her back to him as she mixes their drinks. Positioned directly in front of Eve, the camera shows her continuing to nervously shift her eyes even though we are the only ones who can observe her. The drinks are shared in profile and Eve keeps her head down throughout Thornhill's barbed comments, only once directly meeting his gaze. When she answers the phone, she is shown in profile or with her back to the camera (as opposed to the low angle frontal shot in which Thornhill calls the valet and opens up his full expression to the frame). Eve's attempt to dismiss Thornhill encapsulates the visual dialectic between genuine moment and charade. In a series of close-ups, she begs him to leave and forget about the previous night on the train. Her face is clearly visible, conveying an urgent desire to drive him away from further danger. Once he seems to agree, however, she returns to her casual one-night wonder act and Hitchcock returns to profile and back-to-camera shots. Thornhill's blunt rejection of Eve ("Because I bet you could tease a man to death without half trying. So stop trying, huh?") elicits a medium close-up where Eve's smile fades to an only partially controlled look of hurt.

The stakes are dramatically heightened for Eve at the auction. She must continue to maintain Vandamm's affection, allaying his suspicions and concealing the impact Thornhill's increasingly bitter remarks are having on her. She is seated facing the camera with Vandamm to her side and Thornhill to her back. When Thornhill asks Vandamm if he plans "to ask this *female* to kiss me again and poison me to death," Eve jumps from her seat and tries to strike him with her purse (more on the importance of Eve's handbags later). For a brief moment, she lets everyone see her passion, exchanging her only unguarded gaze with Thornhill and further fanning Vandamm's doubts. Back in her seat, Eve plays only to the camera, and it is only the viewer who sees her brimming tears when Thornhill snipes, "Good night, sweetheart. Don't think it wasn't nice." The tears are revelatory. They convince us finally that Eve's true loyalty is with Thornhill. They prepare and legitimatize the Black Hills rendezvous, the Vandamm hideaway and the Mount Rushmore proposal scenes where Eve and Thornhill freely exchange passionate glances and communicate their genuine love for one another.

The politics of the gaze become complicated in *North by Northwest*. "In a world ordered by sexual imbalance," writes Laura Mulvey, "pleasure in looking has been split between active/male and passive/female. The determining male gaze projects its fantasy onto the female figure, which is styled accordingly. In their traditional exhibitionist role women are simultaneously looked at and displayed, with their appearance coded for strong visual and erotic impact so that they can be said to connote *to-be-looked-at-ness*" (p. 19). Certainly, Eve Kendall is first seen in the film as the object of Roger Thornhill's appreciative glance. Practically rubbing against her when they block each other's path in the train corridor, Thornhill ducks into a compartment to avoid the police and upon re-emerging looks first at Eve, then at the empty corridor and then again at Eve. As she exits to the left of the frame, Thornhill watches her leave, glancing pointedly down at her legs and ankles. A subjective shot from Thornhill's point of view shows Eve's backside as she walks off down the corridor. She is "styled accordingly," in a form-fitting black suit, high heels, pendant necklace, low-cut white silk blouse and sleek black clasp purse. Black elbow length gloves and a black fur wrap ("What becomes a legend most?") over her arm further fetishize her as an expensive object of adorned beauty. A reaction shot shows Thornhill continuing to stare at her until he suddenly remembers his plight and looks out the window to check the position of the cops. Thornhill's various acts of seeing are accentuated by the classic horn-rimmed sunglasses he is wearing.

But briefly here in the film, before her ever-escalating need to conceal her emotions, Eve also wields a powerful sexual gaze. When Thornhill is seated at her table in the dining car, Eve stares so intently at him in a succession of medium shots that he becomes distracted and ill at ease. The continuity script as transcribed by James Naremore details Eve's scrutiny: "She looks directly into Roger's face with evident interest" (p. 83); "She continues looking directly at him and smiles slightly as he adjusts his chair and consults the menu" (p. 83); "The woman sips her coffee and stares at Roger over the rim of the cup" (p. 83); "The woman gazes openly at Roger as he shifts awkwardly in his seat" (p. 84). To regain his composure, Thornhill asks for a menu recommendation, adjusts his sunglasses and, referring to Eve's visual inspection, says that his face must look familiar to her. In a direct allusion to Cary Grant as icon of male beauty, she replies, "It's a nice face." She is unfazed as Thornhill talks about having to guard his desire to make love to attractive women and advises that he shouldn't conceal the impulse since the woman "might not" find it "objectionable." Confessing that she bribed the steward to place Thornhill at her table, Eve takes over as the sexual aggressor. "I never discuss love (re-dubbed from the original 'make love' upon pressure from the Production Code

Administration) on an empty stomach," she tells him just before demolishing his phony introduction as an electronics salesman and promising not to expose him as a notorious wanted murder suspect. With rising innuendo, she notes that "it's going to be a long night" and that "I don't particularly like the book I've started." Boldly and over the span of two protracted close-ups, she looks him directly in the eyes and asks, "Do you know what I mean?"

It is the cigarette lighting (always a heavily coded gesture for Hitchcock) that seals Eve's seduction of Thornhill. As Eve reaches into her purse for a cigarette, Thornhill simultaneously reaches into his pocket for the monogrammed matchbook. A whiff of empty decadence attends Thornhill's admission that the initials "R.O.T." represent his trademark "Rot" and that the "O" stands for "nothing." Neither repelled nor impressed, Eve clasps Thornhill's hand in close-up when it enters the frame from the left with a lighted match. Leaning forward to light the cigarette, Eve keeps hold of Thornhill's hand when it starts to withdraw and then pulls it forward to suggestively blow out the flame. Thornhill gets the message. "I'd invite you to my bedroom," he offers, "if I had a bedroom." Once again, Eve controls events — she gives Thornhill the number of her drawing room and hints that she happens to have an extra pair of pajamas. All of this verbal foreplay occurs during an unprecedented series of almost seventy successive close-ups, camera positions that keep our attention focused on Cary Grant and Eve Marie Saint's hands, eyes and mouths. Eve meets and returns Thornhill's gaze time after time. When the action resumes in Eve's sleeping compartment, she boldly volunteers to "climb up" into the berth where Thornhill is hiding to show him why she is being "so good" to him. It is the same romantic initiative that Eve takes during the Black Hills rendezvous when she suddenly embraces Thornhill and kisses him passionately.

Significantly, of course, Eve's agency and power stem from her exchange value as a sexual commodity. Standing over her at the art auction, Vandamm strokes her neck and hair like the trophy mistress she is and Thornhill refers to her as a "little piece of sculpture" for which Vandamm must have "paid plenty." With Eve seated rigidly between Vandamm and Thornhill against a background of other fine art objects, the two men struggle over her as if placing competing bids on an auction item. During their conversation in the Mount Rushmore cafeteria, Vandamm tells Thornhill he doesn't want "to trade her in for a little piece of mind." Adding to Eve's visual commodification is her tendency to be enclosed in frames like a virtual painting — in the train corridor, against the dining car window, behind the phone booth glass, in the doorway of her hotel room. She is even laid out as an odalisque on her sleeping compartment sofa when the policemen show up to interview her about Thornhill. The camera set-ups, high angle point of view shots from the detectives looking down and low angle ones from Eve looking up, place Eve in a position of vulnerable display, opened up for inspection and evaluation by these two stolid, bland looking American males.

Eve Kendall seduces Roger Thornhill with the lighting of her cigarette.

To the cops, Eve's vamp routine is annoying and highly suspicious, but to the Professor Eve is an important asset. Her "value" is emphasized frequently. "I needn't tell you how valuable she can be to us over there," he tells Thornhill during the forest scene. Earlier, on the Chicago airport tarmac, in reference to her usefulness, he indicated that "much more than her life is at stake." Eve herself remembers that the Professor approached her at the beginning of her affair with Vandamm to argue that she could be "uniquely valuable" to the agency. The Professor is one of three (four counting Hitchcock) older men whom Eve tries hard to please. Both Vandamm and Thornhill are noticeably older than Eve, serving in the combined father figure/love interest roles common to Jimmy Stewart and Cary Grant in the 1950s Hitchcock films. "I'm Eve Kendall. I'm twenty-six and unmarried. Now you know everything," Eve tells Thornhill by way of introduction on the train. The same age as Carlotta Valdes and Madeleine Elster, Eve seems determined to find a wealthy, older partner. "I met Phillip Vandamm at a party one night," she explains to Thornhill after the fake shooting, "and saw only his charm. I guess I had nothing to do that weekend, so I…I decided to fall in love." Moments later, Thornhill asks, "What's wrong with men like me?" and Eve responds, "They don't believe in marriage." In her preoccupation with being comfortably married, Eve is like a brainy and dangerous Lorelei Lee.

Just as Lorelei is always costumed to be at her most alluring, so too is Eve always perfectly packaged and "put together." The departure scene at Vandamm's Mount Rushmore retreat is instructive for the way in which Eve assembles herself. We first see Eve wearing a bright orange, short-sleeved sheath dress with a V-shaped, mixed gem necklace. Later she puts on a matching orange jacket and then just before leaving the house she drapes an orange plaid shawl over her arms and shoulders. By the time she is walking to the airplane, she has added dark silver gloves and a handbag. Except for the intimate scenes in the dining car and hotel room, Eve is continually accessorized with gloves and purse, always for Hitchcock emblematic of a woman's social class and sexual identity (think of the handbags carried by Marion Crane and Melanie Daniels for example). Eve is almost over-dressed for some of the public settings in which she appears; on a summer afternoon, she shows up with Vandamm and Leonard at the Mount Rushmore tourist center wearing a black dress, white pearls, elbow length black gloves, a brown suede handbag and a black cloche hat with brown edging that matches the handbag. Eve must never look anything less than the exotic object of glamour that Hitchcock intends for her to be. As he will later with Tippi Hedren, Hitchcock took special personal interest in Eva Marie Saint's appearance, discarding the M-G-M studio wardrobe designed for her and instead taking her shopping at Bergdorf Goodman. His overall vision was that she "be dressed in a basic black suit (with a simple emerald pendant) to intimate her relationship with [James] Mason; in a heavy silk black cocktail dress subtly imprinted with wine red flowers, in scenes where she deceived Cary; in a charcoal brown, full-skirted jersey and burnt orange burlap outfit in the scenes of action" (McGilligan, p. 567). Relishing his role of fashion Svengali, Hitchcock reportedly bragged, "I've done a great deal for Miss Eva Marie Saint. She was always a good actress, but [in *North by Northwest*] she is no longer the drab, mousy little girl she was. I've given her vitality and sparkle. Now she's a beautiful actress" (p. 567). Ms. Saint's personal feelings notwithstanding,

Hitchcock's remarks have the brusque proprietary tone of something either the Professor or Vandamm might have said about Eve Kendall.

The same meticulous care with which he builds the Eve character is evident as well in the way Hitchcock disassembles her. The prolonged punishment of his too perfect, too secure heroines is an expected narrative arc in Hitchcock's films, played out in the brutal treatment of Madeleine Elster, Marion Crane, Melanie Daniels and Marnie Edgar among others (see Donald Spoto's *Spellbound by Beauty* for insight into Hitchcock's complicated and sometimes tormented relationships in real life with his glamorous leading ladies). And as various feminist film critics have pointed out, assertive women like Eve who dare to return the male gaze are usually punished severely for it. Added to that broad textual factor is Eve's need to atone for entrapping Thornhill, lying to him and sending him off to his near-death in an Indiana cornfield. Once Vandamm discovers her involvement in the phony shooting, she is watched closely and more or less physically constrained. As if walking to her execution, she is escorted to a getaway airplane which appropriately threatens her with death in the same way the crop-duster threatened Thornhill. Fleeing with Thornhill over the Mount Rushmore monument, she is taken apart with the exact step-by-step thoroughness she used to put herself together. First, she snags and abandons her shawl on a branch; next she breaks the heel of a shoe and flings her handbag into the abyss. The final items to be jettisoned are the jacket and what's left of the shoes. She is exposed both physically and psychically, then, when Leonard shoves her off the monument cliff and she dangles in mid air by one gloved hand. Symbolically "resurrected" himself after the staged cafeteria murder, Thornhill controls Eve's fate through the strength of his grip and the strength of his belief in her virtue/value.

Eve is redeemed by her suffering. Hence, the regenerative spiritual imagery associated with her and her religiously freighted first name. A huge flowering tree print dominates the wall above her oversized hotel room bed and a bouquet of white carnations, daisies and gladiolas rests on the dresser. Close to the flowers are two finely carved Buddha statuettes, unusual adornments for a Midwestern hotel room. For the hotel and the auction, Eve herself is dressed in a full black gown with red flowers imprinted across it. The Eve Kendall whom Thornhill lifts upward to safety, transcendence and the marriage she has been seeking is a "chastened" Eve Kendall. Gone are the independence and the assertive roaming gaze; in their place is anchored commitment to a powerful older man capable of dominance in a world controlled by other wealthy white males much like himself.

13: VANDAMMED

Why is Phillip Vandamm so likeable? Both Eve Kendall and the Professor have some ideas. "I met Phillip Vandamm at a party one night," explains Eve by way of back-story, "and saw only his charm." Walking across the runway to catch a flight to Rapid City, the Professor describes Vandamm's espionage operation to Thornhill and concludes, "A rather formidable kind of gentleman, eh?"

First the charm. Sophisticated and intelligent, Vandamm easily navigates the niceties of high culture. He collects art and maintains a modern Frank Lloyd Wright-inspired home at Mount Rushmore. Among his possessions there are piles of strapped and sorted books, probably waiting to be shipped. When he usurps a house for the interrogation of Thornhill, he selects only the best — the Townsend mansion in Glen Cove, New York. His first appearance in the film is smooth and understated. Dressed impeccably in a well cut three-piece suit, he enters the Townsend library unattended by bodyguards, politely greets Thornhill and then proceeds to maneuver around the room, closing draperies and switching on lamps. As the two men circle each other, matching camera pans create a slightly vertiginous effect and set up a visual equivalency between Thornhill and Vandamm. Certainly they are equally handsome and articulate. Ernest Lehman's original script describes Vandamm as "definitely sexually attractive (to women), and only slightly sinister" (p. 11) — an interesting disclaimer intended to abnegate the bisexuality which the rest of the film implies in Vandamm's relationship with Leonard. Vandamm's composure never falters even when Thornhill is unable to provide any information related to Kaplan or U.S. intelligence. In fact, Vandamm's grooming and manners remain perfect throughout the film. He always wears either a sports jacket with tie or a suit in each of his scenes and whether at the art gallery or the Mount Rushmore cafeteria he continues to project a calm, slightly bemused reaction to Thornhill's more histrionic behavior.

His serenity is reinforced by the fact that he is never present when his thugs physically threaten Thornhill; he departs the Townsend library before Thornhill is force fed the bourbon and he leaves the art auction prior to Leonard and Valerian sealing off the exits. As Hitchcock indicates in his interview with Truffaut, Vandamm does not have to carry the full load as villain. "So what we did," explains Hitchcock "was to split the evil character into three people: James Mason, who is attractive and suave; his sinister looking secretary, and the third spy who is crude and brutal" (p. 74).

Vandamm also matches Thornhill in his readiness with a quip. Complimenting Thornhill on his appearance ("Not what I expected. A little taller, a little more polished than the others"), he then adds, "But I'm afraid just as obvious." When Thornhill confronts Eve and Vandamm at the auction regarding Eve's apparent treachery, Vandamm remarks, "Has anyone ever told you that you overplay your various roles rather severely, Mr. Kaplan?" The repartee reflects Vandamm's wit and sarcasm but also his steely sense of superiority and determination, no more so than when Thornhill says, "Apparently the only performance that will satisfy you is when I play dead," and Vandamm replies, "Your very next role. You'll be quite convincing, I assure you." Vandamm's best line, his grace under pressure masterpiece, comes as he and the Professor witness Leonard being shot by one of the troopers who have him in custody, and he declares, as noted earlier, "That wasn't very sporting, using real bullets."

But there is also that formidability which the Professor observed. Remember that Vandamm has ordered the assassination of two of the Professor's best agents before Thornhill comes on the scene. He is running a successful spy ring, and the Professor knows very little about exactly how it operates. Vandamm may not be present for the violence, but he has no problem issuing multiple orders to kill Thornhill. When the drunk driving set-up in "Laura's Mercedes" fails, Vandamm attempts another abduction at the Plaza Hotel, arranges the crop-dusting attack, tries to nab Thornhill at the auction and finally sends Leonard and Valerian climbing over the cliffs of Mount Rushmore to eliminate Thornhill and Eve. In command of some serious resources, Vandamm has a limousine, two sedans, airplanes, a staff of employees and that ultramodern hideaway at his disposal. Toward the end of the film, Vandamm becomes especially forbidding — he punches Leonard in the face after Leonard exposes Eve and then ruthlessly decides that Eve will be killed and ejected from the plane which is set to spirit him out of the country.

Perhaps the major reason for Vandamm's magnetism is that he is portrayed by James Mason. Midway in an impressive career that would ultimately include *Odd Man Out, Five Fingers, Lolita, Georgy Girl* and *The Verdict,* Mason brings his magnificently sonorous voice and his brooding intellectualism to the role of Vandamm. He brings Captain Nemo dismissing his inferiors in *20,000 Leagues Under the Sea,* Erwin Rommel snapping out crisp commands in *The Desert Fox,* Cousin Nicholas cruelly rapping Ann Todd's knuckles in *The Seventh Veil.* But he also imbues Vandamm with the effortless elegance and unanchored melancholy on display in films like *Pandora and the Flying Dutchman* and *A Star is Born.* One of the many pleasures of *North by Northwest* is watching Mason, eyeglasses in one hand and a sheet of paper in the other, read off the destinations from the Kaplan itinerary that Cary Grant as Thornhill denies knowing anything about. "On June the sixteenth," he begins, "you checked into the Sherwyn Hotel in Pittsburgh…[a] week later you registered at the Benjamin Franklin Hotel in Philadelphia…[o]n August the eleventh you stayed at the Statler in Boston." To lessen the tedium of the details, he increases the speed and vehemence of his pronunciation: "On August the twenty-ninth George Kaplan of Boston registered at the Whittier in Detroit [long 'e' and accent on first syllable]. At present, you are registered in room seven ninety-six at the Plaza Hotel in New York…[I]n two days you're due at the Ambassador East in Chicago…and then," speaking as if it is a lunar crater in the Sea of Tranquility, "at the Sheraton-Johnson Hotel in Rapid City, South Dakota," each syllable of the city and state receiving an equally firm and aggrieved emphasis. It is the exact cadence Mason uses for his emotional "I need a job" speech during the Academy Awards scene of *A Star is Born.* James Mason is so commanding as Phillip Vandamm that it is hard to believe Hitchcock originally wanted Yul Brynner for the role when the character was called "Mendoza."

Commenting on Mason's early career in Britain, David Thomson has written, "But he really came to the fore during the war years in a run of films where he brought a unique sensuality to polite arrogance" (p. 571). Both qualities are still there in his Vandamm performance. The sensuality is clear as he stalks the Townsend library in semi-darkness, the polite arrogance as he mocks Thornhill, "Games? Must we?" In her review of *Lolita,* Pauline Kael refers to how Mason's "handsome face gloats in a rotting smile" (p. 207). And that attractively yet thinly disguised menace is there in Vandamm also, particularly in the auction scene where he strains to maintain his civility while seething with jealousy and disdain toward Thornhill.

Vandamm is not the first of Hitchcock's sympathetic villains. Counterparts include Uncle Charlie in *Shadow of a Doubt*, Norman Bates in *Psycho* and, particularly, Alex Sebastian in *Notorious*. Both Sebastian and Vandamm are wealthy gentlemen, foreign spies and the losing corners of complicated love triangles. Both are the more cultured foils to initially unlikeable "heroes" played in both films by Cary Grant. Therein lies the dynamic that Hitchcock is after — characters who are neither completely good nor completely evil. The films may be thoroughly unrealistic and illogical but the world view has realistic resonance to it. Unalloyed good does not exist in Hitchcock's universe (even niece Charlie in *Shadow of a Doubt* is judgmental and self-righteous), and viewers have to work harder than with most Hollywood films in anchoring their loyalties. Unlike Eve, we may not see only Vandamm's charm at first, but to see any of it is to admit our own ambiguous morality.

14: WHAT ABOUT LEONARD?

It is clear that Phillip Vandamm's personal secretary Leonard is gay. We are way more certain about Leonard, in fact, than we are about the muddlingly portrayed Sebastian Venable in *Suddenly, Last Summer*, another big name film released in 1959. Leonard talks about his "woman's intuition," dangles his legs coquettishly when sitting on a table at the art gallery and fusses with his hair a lot. Leonard's first appearance in the film is when he slides into the library and, after quickly cruising Thornhill, says approvingly, "He's a well-tailored one, isn't he?"

The stage directions in Ernest Lehman's original script are even more explicit about Leonard: "He is about thirty, but looks much younger, for he has a soft baby-face, large eyes, and hair that falls down over his forehead. His attitudes are unmistakably feminine" (p. 11). As written by Lehman and played by Martin Landau, Leonard is a gunsel, à la Elisha Cook, Jr. in *The Maltese Falcon*.

But if Leonard's attitude is unmistakably feminine, the film's attitude is unmistakably homophobic. Leonard comes with decades' worth of gay stereotypes attached. Misogynistic and predatory, Leonard is the one who rifles through Eve's luggage, discovers the blank cartridges and exposes her as a double agent. Once he learns that Vandamm plans to eliminate Eve during the transoceanic flight, Leonard can barely contain his sadistic pleasure; "it would please me if you would think of me as being along on this journey…if only in spirit," he tells Eve as they all await the plane's landing. So far beyond the norms of basic human decency is Leonard that he first refuses to help Thornhill pull Eve back from the Mount Rushmore cliff and then proceeds to brutally grind Thornhill's fingers with his shoe as Thornhill himself dangles from the edge.

The equation of Leonard's homosexuality with his traitorous espionage serves to reinforce his estrangement from the "normal" American life led by Roger Thornhill. He is twice over the "other" and must be doubly mistrusted. As the perverse outsider he reflects a tendency traced by Vito Russo's *The Celluloid Closet* in films "through the Fifties to define gays as aliens" (p. 94). When present in mid-century movies at all, gays are portrayed either as buffoonish sissies like Franklin Pangborn and Grady Sutton or as traitors, killers and deviants. Leonard takes his place as a deadly sissy in the tradition of Waldo Lydecker in *Laura* and Joel Cairo in

Leonard casts a jealous and spiteful glance at Eve Kendall.

The Maltese Falcon, and his sexual interest in Thornhill is designed to make him even more unsavory. "Later, we will see him at closer range," suggest the original script directions, "and perhaps be slightly repelled" (p. 11). When Leonard remarks on Thornhill's appearance, the script indicates that "Thornhill gives him a look of distaste" (p. 12). (The lathered passenger in the La Salle Street station men's room gives Thornhill a similar look, played for laughs, as he watches Thornhill use Eve's mini razor to shave his morning beard.) Again Russo, commenting on films of the 60s, is instructive on this element of Leonard's characterization: "Although, under the new code, villainous homosexuals sometimes wanted the hero sexually, their homosexuality served as an illustration of their pathology and thus illuminated their villainy" (p. 133).

Leonard is not Hitchcock's first gay character. Predecessors include Philip Morgan and Brandon Shaw in *Rope*, Bruno Anthony in *Strangers on a Train*, Handel Fane in *Murder!* and probably Uncle Charlie in *Shadow of a Doubt* and Norman Bates in *Psycho*. Critics have argued at length about whether Norman in particular is gay, bisexual, cross-gendered, misogynistically heterosexual or even asexual but clearly he is like the other Hitchcock "deviants" in his alienation from society and his variance from the straight male norm. To this group I would add butch female villains like Mrs. Danvers in *Rebecca*, Madame Sebastian in *Notorious* and Valerian's housekeeper wife in *North by Northwest*. In *Flaming Classics: Queering the Film Canon*, Alexander Doty argues convincingly that every one of Hitchcock's treacherous psychopaths is sexually questionable. "I am willing to concede," he writes, "that not all of Hitchcock's psychos are clearly or consistently coded as homosexual, largely as a result of cultural and film censorship practices in England and America, but I defy anyone to point to a Hitchcock psychopath who is clearly and consistently presented as a conventionally masculine heterosexual. No, I am not confusing gender and sexuality here. Within a traditional patriarchal perspective, to be questionably 'masculine' is almost always to be sexually 'suspect' to some degree" (p. 165).

"I know how terribly fond you are of Miss Kendall," Leonard tells Vandamm just before exposing Eve's betrayal. "Terribly fond"? How about "passionately in love with"? But sexual passion is not really part of Vandamm's feelings toward Eve Kendall. Unlike Thornhill, who enfolds Eve in a prolonged gymnastic kiss in the 20th Century Limited sleeping car, Vandamm never embraces Eve. Instead he treats her like a trophy, as he does at the art gallery when he possessively grasps her by the back of the neck. Eve is part of his art collection, a stylish and sophisticated beard allowing him to move smoothly through cultured society in the same way that another Eve (the titular Miss Harrington) does for Addison DeWitt in *All about Eve*.

Vandamm spends most of his time with Leonard. It is Leonard who helps with the Townsend mansion interrogation of Thornhill and who tellingly spends the night with Vandamm in their shared compartment aboard the train to Chicago. In fact there is no scene featuring Vandamm, whether it be the art gallery, the Mount Rushmore cafeteria or the cliffside hideaway, that does not also include Leonard. Aware of Leonard's devotion and believing it to be the cause of Leonard's suspicion of Eve, Vandamm teasingly tells him, "You know what I think? I think you're jealous. No, I mean it. I'm very touched. Very."

Russo states that Vandamm and Leonard maintain a "covert homosexual relationship" (p. 94), but Vandamm's narrative function exceeds even that categorization. He is as handsome and debonair as Thornhill, more cultured and definitely more cosmopolitan, but his politics are anti-American and his sexuality is ambivalent and polymorphous. His example cannot stand as a morally legitimate alternative. His capture along with Leonard's death prepares the way for the formation of a traditional heterosexual couple and the re-establishment of a straight status quo. Closing their film with Thornhill and Eve's wedding night embrace, Hitchcock and Lehman definitively signal that society has been made safe once again for American capitalism and for heterosexual marriage.

15: SPY VS. SPY

Ian Fleming wrote *Casino Royale*, the first book in the James Bond series, in 1953. Graham Greene published *The Quiet American* in 1955 and *Our Man in Havana* in 1958. With *Pickup on South Street* (1953) and *Kiss Me Deadly* (1955), Sam Fuller and Robert Aldrich blended *film noir* style with plots involving Russian agents, nuclear secrets and domestic espionage. The newspapers and magazines were also full of real-life spy stories. Guy Burgess and Donald Maclean had defected from England to the Soviet Union in 1951, and Julius and Ethel Rosenberg were convicted and executed in 1953 on their extremely controversial espionage charge. Raising the international stakes, Soviet troops were sent in to suppress the Budapest uprising in 1956, and in 1958 Kruschev initiated the Berlin Crisis with demands regarding governance of the two German states and access to West Berlin.

North by Northwest's tale of agents and double agents plotting to secure secret microfilm fits naturally into this Zeitgeist of Cold War tension. There is even a direct reference in *North by Northwest* to Whittaker Chambers's microfilm laden pumpkin when Thornhill rescues Eve outside Vandamm's house and says, "I see you've got the pumpkin," indicating her possession of the statue used to conceal Vandamm's microfilm. Additionally, Hitchcock, beginning with the British sound films, had long favored the spy genre probably because it so easily accommodated his recurrent themes of complacency, deception, victimization, betrayal, the violation of private space and the illusory stability of power and position. Prior to *North by Northwest*, he directed nine films about espionage: *The 39 Steps*, *Secret Agent*, *Sabotage*, *The Lady Vanishes*, *Foreign Correspondent*, *Saboteur*, *Notorious* and both versions of *The Man Who Knew Too Much*. In fact, as discussed in earlier chapters, *North by Northwest* combines the innocent man on the run motif of *The 39 Steps* with Cary Grant's déjà-vu dilemma from *Notorious* of watching the woman he loves forced by her U.S. intelligence assignment to become the mistress of a foreign spy. After *North by Northwest,* Hitchcock would return to the world of international intrigue in *Torn Curtain* and *Topaz*. Improving on the Technicolor sheen and picturesque locales of the second *The Man Who Knew Too Much*, *North by Northwest* prefigures the exotic travelogue action of the 007 films. So too does Vandamm's debonair and sophisticated antagonist become a model for the cultured Bond movie villains. Think Karl Stromberg or Hugo Drax but without James Mason's unique good looks and voice. Leo G. Carroll, who as recently as 1955 was getting menaced by a giant spider in *Tarantula,* revived his career as the Professor, creating the avuncular intelligence agency chief role that he would successfully reprise as Alexander Waverly in NBC's *The Man from U.N.C.L.E* television series (1964-68).

Besides enhancing overall production values, *North by Northwest* gives us much more interesting characters than does *The Man Who Knew Too Much*. Cary Grant and Eva Marie Saint are a more stylish and erotically plausible couple than James Stewart and Doris Day. They are the Kennedys to Stewart and Day's Dick and Pat Nixon. While both Grant and Stewart are involuntarily drawn into intrigue, Stewart's Dr. Ben McKenna is merely pissed off and bossy; Thornhill's psychological baggage is way more complex. And where Doris Day's Jo McKenna is steadfastly loyal to husband and son, Eve Kendall is morally compromised and racked by conflicting loyalties.

Even though he is not a trained secret agent, Roger Thornhill reacts to danger with a kind of irreverent nonchalance. Steady under pressure, he is quick with a quip and a comeback. When the housekeeper and Valerian discuss where in the Glen Cove mansion to confine Thornhill in light of the arriving dinner guests, he asks, "By the way, what are we having for dessert?" As Valerian leaves him locked in the library, he says, "Don't hurry. I'll catch up on my reading." Most sarcastically of all, he comes upon Vandamm, Leonard and Eve at the Chicago art auction after narrowly escaping death in the crop-dusting attack and remarks, "Now that's a picture only Charles Addams could draw." It is this same penchant for slightly snarky one-liners that is used to good effect by Sean Connery in *Goldfinger*, stretched to painful extremes by Roger Moore, mercifully put to rest by Daniel Craig and, in between, mimicked widely by James Coburn as Derek Flint, Dean Martin as Matt Helm and Robert Vaughn as Napoleon Solo.

Under the glamour and humor of *North by Northwest*, however, lies a disenchantment with the business of spying. Clearly the Professor and his United States Intelligence Agency colleagues care little for the safety of

Roger Thornhill and not much more for that of their own double agent Eve Kendall. At the staff meeting in which they review how Thornhill ended up mistaken for their non-existent decoy agent George Kaplan, the comments range from "c'est la guerre" to "if it's so horribly sad, how is it I feel like laughing?" When Mrs. Finlay suggests that they might be "callous" in not intervening to save Thornhill, the Professor testily argues that the mission must remain supreme and that they can't risk the "suspicion, exposure and assassination" of their own agent. That agent is Eve Kendall, but the Professor is even willing to put her life in danger when he decides in Rapid City that she should accompany Vandamm out of the country even though Vandamm is beginning to seriously question her loyalty and love.

Thornhill's disagreement with the Professor regarding Eve's undercover assignment contains the film's strongest indictment of the murky ethics that permeate intelligence gathering. "I don't like the games you play," Thornhill tells the Professor. Refusing to accept the Professor's condescending "War is hell, Mr. Thornhill, even when it's a cold one" response, Thornhill angrily argues, "If you fellows can't lick the Vandamms of this world without asking girls like her to bed down with them and fly away with them and probably never come back, perhaps you ought to start learning how to lose a few cold wars." "I'm afraid we're already doing that," says the Professor.

The Professor and the South Dakota State troopers ultimately apprehend Vandamm and shoot Leonard but only because Thornhill has forced the situation and because there are no other viable options. We are left with a sour taste regarding the Professor's dispassionate pursuit of national security. Our mistrust is extended by the carefully composed establishing shot which begins the Professor's conference scene. By opening on an engraved building plaque which reads "United States Intelligence Agency" and which reflects an image of the Capitol on its shiny surface, Hitchcock suggests that the Professor's questionable tactics extend outward as a normal part of government operations.

North by Northwest, then, marks a kind of transition in Hitchcock's treatment of espionage. The Professor is a far cry from the matronly piano playing master spy Miss Froy in *The Lady Vanishes* but not yet at the level of brutality and official international deception that characterize the late 60s films *Torn Curtain* and *Topaz*. Changing the whole tenor of the spy genre after 1959 will be the work of John Le Carré, who will publish *The Spy Who Came in from the Cold* in 1963 and see it adapted for the screen in 1965.

16: "A CARY GRANT PICTURE"

A select handful of favorite actors starred for Alfred Hitchcock in multiple films — Tippi Hedren and Farley Granger in two each, Grace Kelly and Ingrid Bergman in three and Jimmy Stewart and Cary Grant in a record-setting four (*North by Northwest's* Professor, Leo G. Carroll, worked six times for Hitchcock but only in supporting roles). Stewart and Grant appear in several of the films most closely associated with Hitchcock, including *Notorious, Rear Window, Vertigo, To Catch a Thief* and, of course, *North by Northwest*. As such, the two actors give Hitchcock the opportunity to spin endless variations on his double-sided hero paradigm: Stewart the prosaic somewhat petulant everyman struggling to survive his flaws and Grant the impossibly debonair charmer maneuvering to conceal his flaws.

Even more so than Stewart in *Vertigo*, Cary Grant dominates *North by Northwest*. Appearing in all but the brief Intelligence Agency conference scene, Grant is on screen for almost the entire 136 minute running time. Screenwriter Ernest Lehman was well aware that he was writing a film tailored to Grant's special talents as well as Hitchcock's interests and remembers lively arguments with Grant about the plot's improbabilities: "He would sit there and go over some of his scenes with me. 'This is ridiculous,' he'd say, 'You think you are writing a Cary Grant picture? This is a David Niven picture'" (Naremore, p. 5). It is hard to imagine Niven or any comparable Hollywood actor, however, bringing to the role the humor, subtlety, athleticism and sexiness that Grant delivers. For Hitchcock and for Hawks, Cary Grant did some of his finest work ever.

Various aspects of Grant's screen persona come together seamlessly in the Thornhill portrayal. Present are the action hero of *Only Angels Have Wings* and *Gunga Din*, the brash manipulator of *His Girl Friday*, the farceur of *Bringing Up Baby* and *Monkey Business* and the slightly dangerous romantic lead of *The Talk of the Town* and *The Philadelphia Story*. The very public embarrassment that Grant suffers in *I Was a Male War Bride* is reprised repeatedly in *North by Northwest* as Thornhill is laughed at by fellow passengers in the Plaza elevator, blamed by the crowd for the United Nations murder and ogled by tourists when he is "shot" in the Mount Rushmore cafeteria. Grant is able to make us believe and care about Thornhill's change from a cocky executive who filches cabs to a sympathetic victim in need of assistance. And, evoking the French characters he played in *War Bride* and *To Catch a Thief*, Grant easily matches gesture for gesture and syllable for syllable the cosmopolitan urbanity that James Mason expresses as foreign agent Phillip Vandamm.

Review his four different Hitchcock parts and Grant's range as an actor becomes extremely apparent. As Johnnie Aysgarth in *Suspicion*, he lies, cheats, steals and makes Joan Fontaine believe he is trying to kill her (which he would have if RKO had been willing to fully adapt the Francis Iles source material). Drawing on his Bristol childhood and playing the same British cad he covers in *None but the Lonely Heart*, Grant shifts back and forth from brooding anger to manic exuberance. In *Notorious* he is even darker, creating what is probably his most morally ambiguous characterization. Made four years after he became a United States citizen, *Notorious* casts Grant as the extremely American, extremely laconic, government intelligence agent T.R. Devlin. Following orders, he pressures Ingrid Bergman into spying on Nazi conspirator Claude Rains and then blames her for marrying him as part of the cover. He is torn by jealousy, love and anger, moving from an embrace to a scowl in the same scene. Grant's trademark coolness here becomes coldness as he bites off cutting insults to Bergman and watches her with narrowed judgmental eyes. You can see the resentment toward his superiors flickering beneath Devlin's diplomacy, and Grant brings it to flashpoint in a brilliant throwaway scene where he lashes out at some hypocritical governmental officials for referring to Bergman as a "woman of that sort" whom they are content to let do the dirty work while their wives "of great honor and virtue" play bridge in Washington. Grant is even able to make Devlin's eleventh hour reversal of attitude believable when he comes upon the poisoned, almost comatose, Bergman and whispers rapid assurances of love to make up for months of spiteful neglect.

To Catch a Thief showcases the glamour of Cary Grant. This is Cote d'Azur Cary, America's ideal image of itself abroad, confident amid European wealth, fluent in French, elegant in whatever he wears whether it be black tie or crewneck sweaters and espadrilles. Grant's effortless physicality highlights his portrayal of former cat burglar John Robie.

Calling on the skills of former acrobat Archie Leach, Grant clambers over steep tiled roofs, swims the Mediterranean and races cars along the Corniche. He underplays the part perfectly, reacting to Grace Kelly's sexual aggressiveness with hesitant restraint and bemused irony. *To Catch a Thief* is a lighter, lesser Hitchcock movie carried, as his final films never could be, by an actor interesting to watch for the way he moves on screen, the way he animates a close-up. As already mentioned, *North by Northwest* encompasses both the physical and the interior dimensions of Grant's acting. He transitions easily from the broad slapstick comedy of the drunken jailhouse scene to the witty repartee of the dining car seduction, from the stunned regret of the tarmac conversation to the moral indignation of the Black Hills forest rendezvous. The crop-dusting attack is a fine example of Grant's subtle skills. Nominally an action piece, the scene's tension and viewer involvement come also from what Grant is able to do in close-up with just his face and his gestures. Throughout what is basically a ten minute segment of silent cinema, Grant suggests frustration with the slouch of his shoulders, alertness with the tentative removal of his hands from his pockets and indecision with a wrinkled brow and a bitten lower lip. Nothing is forced nor over the top, not even the rapidly cut climax (of panicked facial expressions and waving arms) in which Grant is nearly run over by a ten wheeler truck.

And, of course, there is also the sexual chemistry that Grant has been able to sustain with an amazing, decades-spanning list of actresses that includes Mae West, Marlene Dietrich, Carole Lombard, Tallulah Bankhead, Sylvia Sidney, Loretta Young, Katharine Hepburn, Myrna Loy, Jean Harlow, Irene Dunne, Joan Bennett, Constance Bennett, Jean Arthur, Rosalind Russell, Ginger Rogers, Ingrid Bergman, Ann Sheridan, Jeanne Crain, Deborah Kerr, Grace Kelly, Sophia Loren, Doris Day, Leslie Caron and Audrey Hepburn. Again the comparison with Stewart is instructive. In *The Philadelphia Story*, both of them play off the mannered dynamo that is Katharine Hepburn; Stewart's awkwardness around her is countered by Grant's looseness. In their Hitchcock films with Grace Kelly, Stewart resists the future Princess's full-of-herself romantic allure while Grant mocks and parries it. Grant's comfort as romantic leading man is there in *North by Northwest* as well. He watches Eva Marie Saint walk down a train corridor and suggestively light a cigarette with surprise and appreciation. When she seduces him over a dinner of brook trout, he responds with a somewhat skeptical sense of playfulness. To what could otherwise be the conventional down time in a romantic thriller he brings a full emotional arc that moves through infatuation, anger, jealousy and protectiveness.

As in *Notorious*, there is a sustained single take embrace in which Grant and Saint rotate against the wall of a sleeping compartment and project a sensuality made even more amazing by the fact that they are both still fully clothed in business dress.

Cary Grant is in total movie star mode in *North by Northwest* and both he and Hitchcock play with his celebrity persona. As the fugitive Thornhill, he dons a pair of sunglasses to disguise himself in Grand Central Station and is wearing them when he literally bumps into Eve Kendall on board the Chicago-bound train. "I know. I look vaguely familiar," he tells her later in the dining car. "You feel you've seen me somewhere before…Funny how I have that effect on people. It's something about my face." Responding like a fan, she replies, "It's a nice face." Cary Grant playing Roger Thornhill draws a similar fan reaction when he sneaks through a hospital room and the female patient turns on the light, puts on her glasses, gets a good look at Grant and first alarmingly and then ardently implores him to "stop!" It's the same kind of self-reflexive, subtextual humor that Grant expresses when he asks Officer Flamm at the Chicago airport, "Does anyone mind if I sit down? I've been running all day." At age 55, Grant is completely believable as a romantic action hero, so convincing that apparently Ian Fleming wanted him to play 007 when *Dr. No* was filmed three years later since he had had Grant in mind when he created James Bond in the first place. Grant refused, saying he was then too old, even though in 1963 he basically replayed the same part in Stanley Donen's Hitchcock influenced *Charade* where he was a very credible romantic interest for Audrey Hepburn, who at thirty-three was a quarter of a century younger than he was.

Grant's consummate skill in legitimizing this kind of character is emphasized by all those who have failed to pull off the challenge — among them, Paul Newman in *Torn Curtain*, Rock Hudson in *Blindfold* and, most recently, Johnny Depp in *The Tourist*. The refusal of Cary Grant's colleagues to recognize his artistry is one of Hollywood's most shameful oversights. Nominated for an Academy Award as Best Actor only in 1941 (*Penny Serenade*) and 1944 (*None But the Lonely Heart*), he lost both times, to Gary Cooper in *Sergeant York* and Bing Crosby in *Going My Way* respectively. In 1959, when he should have been nominated for *North by Northwest*, the honorees were Laurence Harvey in *Room at the Top*, Jack Lemmon in *Some Like it Hot*, Paul Muni in *The Last Angry Man*, James Stewart in *Anatomy of a Murder* and ultimate winner Charlton Heston in *Ben-Hur*. Cary Grant, along with Robert Mitchum, is the most undervalued actor of Hollywood's Golden Age. The nearest female equivalent is

Barbara Stanwyck, and she failed to win an Oscar probably for the same reason as Grant. Neither star ever signed a long-term studio contract and consequently never had the benefit of block voting when Academy Awards were decided. To make up for its slight, the Academy gave Grant an honorary Oscar in 1970 just as it did for Stanwyck in 1982. People will be watching Cary Grant in his Hawks films, his Hitchcock films and even his Leo McCarey comedies, however, long after many of his Oscar winning contemporaries have been forgotten. David Thomson gets it exactly right in *The New Biographical Dictionary of Film* when he writes, "There is a major but very difficult realization that needs to be reached about Grant — difficult, that is, for many people who like to think they take the art of film seriously. As well as being a leading box-office draw for some thirty years…he was the best and most important actor in the history of cinema" (p. 351).

17: THE SUIT

No other item of male clothing in American film history has the iconic status of Cary Grant's gray suit and tie in *North by Northwest*. What comes close? Bogart's white dinner jacket or raincoat in *Casablanca*? Travolta's white suit and vest in *Saturday Night Fever*? Lancaster's swim trunks in *From Here to Eternity*? Maybe, but none is as omnipresent in the film, as emblematic of the character, nor as flawlessly, fundamentally stylish as the gray suit. The most illustrative equivalent is Audrey Hepburn's black Givenchy in *Breakfast at Tiffany's* or the strapless black satin Jean Louis gown that Rita Hayworth wears for the "Put the Blame on Mame" number in *Gilda*. Like the dresses, Grant's suit is timeless. And like the dresses, it operates on the level of characterization, the object reflecting an essential aspect of the protagonist. In Saussurian terms, the suit signifies on multiple levels, conveying Thornhill's identity as an assured New Yorker and then as a consummate, appropriately uniformed ad executive (reflective of Sloan Wilson's 1955 *The Man in the Gray Flannel Suit*) and finally, on a mystic level, Cary Grant's identity as debonair, age-defying Hollywood male film star.

The suit is, of course, bespoke, but there is considerable disagreement over the tailor (Norton and Sons, Quintino, Kilgour?), the color (gray or blue), the pattern (plain or checked), the cut (pleats? vents?) and the fabric (13 oz. flannel or 10 oz. tropical weave). Complicating the issue is the fact that several suits were used during production to enable Grant to get seriously mussed up during the jail, the train berth and the crop duster scenes and still look perfectly groomed walking into the Shaw and Oppenheim Galleries and the Mount Rushmore cafeteria. The color quality and resolution of various film prints make a definitive color identification difficult as well, and some publicity and lobby photos alter the color along with the pattern even more dramatically.

I believe that final authority on the suit's structural details rests with Chris Laverty, creator of the "Clothes on Film" blog, and Richard

Torregrossa, author of *Cary Grant: A Celebration of Style*. Laverty describes Thornhill's basic ensemble as "lightweight wool single breasted suit, ventless, with three button fastening and notched labels. Trousers with forward pleats. 'Oxblood' leather derby shoes worn with grey thin ribbed socks. White medium spread collar shirt with double cuff; silver cufflinks; grey silk tie" (Laverty).

Laverty and Torregrossa agree that the suit is a subtle glen-plaid and is blue on a gray background. The dual color checked pattern is particularly clear when Cary stands next to James Mason's plain light gray suit in the auction scene. Mistaking the color, says Torregrossa "is understandable because on screen it certainly appears to be a mid-gray, largely the result of the intense lighting that softens or at time eradicates fine details" (Torregrossa). Torregrossa suggests that "another reason for the suit's grey appearance is that its blend of colors and glen-plaid pattern resolve in long shots to a luminous but seemingly solid hue in very much the same way the brush strokes in a Monet painting became less evident and the image more sharply focused when you step back from it" (Torregrossa).

Laverty and Torregrossa also agree that the suit is the product of Kilgour, French and Stanbury of Savile Row in London. "Specifically," adds Laverty, "it was tailored by Arthur Lyons (who also made suits for Edward, Duke of Windsor). The trousers are cut high for Grant's typical waistband, fitting loose through the seat and thigh" (Laverty). In one of the endless chatroom debates about the suit, Lyon's grandson Derek confirmed that his grandfather tailored the suit at Kilgour.

The suit's design is an essential scaffolding within the mise-en-sène. It accommodates Grant's unique gesturality, facilitating his trademark postures, movements and attitudes. The perfect upper body fit devoid of neck-roll conceals Grant's slightly rounded shoulders and concave chest, giving him that virile athleticism essential to the national cultural code he embodies here. The full cut pants and the extended length to the jacket allow Grant to stride smoothly and confidently across the Plaza Hotel lobby, his long legs accented like a dancer's in a seamless piece of fluid sculpture. And cutting the jacket high alongside the pants pockets allows Grant, by leaving undone the bottom button of his unvented jacket, to thrust his hands into his side pockets (without crumpling and bunching the jacket) for that characteristically casual grace under pressure pose he strikes while standing on the side of Highway 41.

The deceptively simple sack suit that Roger Thornhill selects from his well stocked closet that day in October and wears from New York to Chicago to South Dakota has had a resilient and wide-reaching influence.

The November 2006 issue of *GQ* placed it at the top of its list of the 25 best examples of men's clothing in international cinema. Also in the top five were the clothes from *Breathless, Ocean's 11, Purple Noon* and *8 1/2*. For its 2006 Hollywood issue, *Vanity Fair* restaged several classic Hitchcock scenes with contemporary actors and placed Seth Rogen (a curious choice) in the suit for the shot of Thornhill running at the camera with the crop-dusting plane diving in low behind him (photographed near Carpenteria, California, this time and not near Bakersfield). Tom Cruise wore a version of the suit in *Collateral* as did Ben Affleck in *Paycheck*. And in the summer 2006 issue of *Granta,* Todd McEwen wrote a humorous essay titled "Cary Grant's Suit," in which he recounts each of the ordeals the suit endures and survives. James Cromwell later recorded a complete reading of the essay for NPR.

Although McEwen is mostly interested in the comic disparity between how bloodied, soiled and shredded the suit should be and how pristinely groomed it and Cary magically remain, he is actually very insightful about the way in which the suit mirrors Thornhill's sense of self. "The title sequence," he comments, "in which the stark lines of a Madison Avenue office building are 'woven' together could be the construction of Cary in his suit right there — he gets knitted into his suit, into his job, before our eyes…Cary's suit reflects New York, identifies him as a thrusting exec, but also arms him, protects him: what else is a suit for? Reflects and Protects: a slogan Cary's character, Roger Thornhill, might have come up with himself" (McEwen). It is exactly this cocky complacency for which Thornhill will be punished. When his security is shattered, he is forced into a journey to get it back (to be worthy of wearing the suit again, according to McEwen) and as we've seen with heroic quests, interest lies in whether he has the necessary instincts and talents to succeed and whether he learns anything transformative in the process.

18: "DUSTIN' CROPS"

North by Northwest's crop-dusting scene is one of cinema's great set pieces, deserving of pantheon placement along with *Battleship Potemkin's* Odessa Steps massacre, the *Casablanca* airport farewell and *Touch of Evil's* opening tracking shot. Spanning nearly ten minutes of screen time, the scene is comprised of some 130 separate shots and contains only fourteen brief lines of dialogue. It is essentially a validation of silent cinema, a tribute to the power of montage to control emotion and generate suspense.

As shaped by Lehman and Hitchcock, the crop-dusting episode is also a classically crafted film within a film. It has a beginning, middle and end; it has rising action, a climax, a denouement. Viewed from a strictly pragmatic perspective, the Prairie Stop segment makes almost no logical sense. Why would Vandamm go to such trouble and expense to eliminate Thornhill when a simple hit outside the La Salle Street Station would suffice? Why would the crop-dusting plane fly directly at the tanker truck once Thornhill has flagged it down? Why wouldn't the truck-jacked farmer just borrow a car from one of the other onlookers and chase after Thornhill? Considered, however, for its iteration of visual images and narrative patterns present in the rest of the film, the scene is organically essential and meaningful.

Ernest Lehman has admitted cooking up the crop-dusting gimmick with Hitchcock one afternoon in the director's study. From Hitchcock's original even more preposterous idea of a cyclone threatening Thornhill, the skyborne menace became a plane "dustin' crops where there ain't no crops." A shot-by-shot analysis based on repeat viewings of the 2010 TCM DVD, the Rutgers shooting script and the Albert LaValley storyboard published in *Focus on Hitchcock* reveals the multiple levels of meaning and signification present in the incident at Prairie Stop:

1. Extreme long shot. A close-up of Eve Kendall's face dissolves into a high-angle aerial of Highway 41 cutting diagonally from the left horizon to the lower right corner of the frame. Eve has set Thornhill up for this meeting, and so her image hovers like a foreboding spirit over the new geography. Upon the dissolve, the non-diegetic music ends, emphasizing the silence and emptiness of this place. A dirt road intersects the highway to create quadrants reminiscent of the grid like design of the opening credits. A Greyhound bus appears, proceeds to mid frame and discharges Roger Thornhill. (A major advertiser on American network television at the time ["take the bus and leave the driving to us"], Greyhound was considered a respectable middle-class means of transportation.) As the bus disappears from the bottom of the frame, Thornhill stands alone amid his vast surroundings, diminished by the immensity. At a little over 50 seconds, this will be by far the longest held shot in the entire Prairie Stop sequence. Like an adagio, it is stillness before upheaval.

2. Long shot. From ground level, Thornhill is positioned against the left side of the frame, seeming to merge with the fence posts. A white sign identifies the road as Highway 41. All around Thornhill there is only blank sky and flat brown horizon. Part of a wider modernist context, the landscape evokes Eliot's Wasteland and Fitzgerald's Valley of the Ashes. Thornhill turns to his right in the direction of the departing Greyhound.

3. Long shot. Matching his gaze, the eye line cut takes us to a point of view (POV) shot of the bus as it disappears in the distance. With his first use here of subjective camera, Hitchcock builds our identification with Thornhill. Within a three shot arc, we have gone from distanced bird's-eye objectivity to an intimately shared feeling of vulnerability.

4. Medium shot. Thornhill stands in front of the marker looking first to the left and then to the right. Indicating only a highway number and a bus stop, the signage is intentionally vague and devoid of state or city reference points. We could be in any barren dreamscape. Uncertain of how to proceed, Thornhill clasps his hands in front of his body.

5. Long shot. Another subjective POV and another diagonal composition. An empty field with posts and the shoulder of the highway as seen by Thornhill.

6-11. A series of three medium shots of Thornhill staring into space followed by three reaction long shots of the empty fields and highway he is observing. Thornhill is like a human antenna, pivoting in a 360° sweep to find signs of life. But the isolation is complete. In a gesture of restless uncertainty that Thornhill displays throughout the film, he shoves his hands into the side pockets of his pants. When he looks left across the highway, Thornhill glimpses a parched cornfield on the horizon. In one of the POV shots, Hitchcock shows us a crop-dusting plane flying in the far background of the frame. Both shots are examples of Hitchcock planting details that later will dramatically impact the action.

12. Medium shot. Thornhill looks again to the right. Cued by the repetitions, we assume that Thornhill's gaze soon will yield something significant. A feature film's real time conventions, we know, are different from those of a modern theatre piece; waiting for Kaplan, then, should be less interminable than waiting for Godot.

2. Thornhill is isolated in open space against the stark vertical fenceposts.

13. Long shot. From Thornhill's POV, a car appears in the distance. There are no visual prompts to indicate whether this will be a positive or a negative development.

14. Medium shot. Anticipating change, Thornhill lifts his shoulders and braces his posture. Cary Grant, the former acrobat and stilt walker, deftly uses body language to convey Thornhill's vacillating sense of expectation.

15. Long shot. A white convertible speeds past as the camera pans to follow it exiting frame left. The car's top is up and the windows are sealed, emphasizing the day's intense heat and further separating Thornhill from human contact. Reminiscent of a dream's vague peripheral details, the occupant(s) cannot be clearly distinguished. For the first time since the braking and accelerating of the bus, silence is momentarily interrupted and then heightened by the passing whir of the convertible's high horsepower engine.

16-20. In the familiar alternation between medium shots and POV long shots, Thornhill watches the car disappear, glances to the right and then looks back again to his left. Hitchcock's sustained use of the subjective camera foregrounds his technique and asserts his presence even more directly than the opening credit cameo. Since the departure of the Greyhound, no shot has been held longer than about five seconds and the consistent *plein américain* camera height keeps us firmly anchored to the earth with Thornhill. Form as much as content is generating tension.

21. Long Shot. A dark car materializes on the opposite horizon from where the convertible approached. Color coding suggests this may be a more ominous appearance.

22. Medium shot. Thornhill tightens his gaze. "The secret is people's faces," John Ford remarked on the key to appreciating film performances, "their eye expression, their movement" (McBride, p. 2). Cary Grant projects a complex mix of anxiety, concern, anticipation and hope with just his eyes.

23. Long shot. As opposed to the convertible, the dark car approaches more slowly, a possible sign that this is "Kaplan."

24. Medium shot. Same camera position as 23. Thornhill straightens his body and begins to slide his hands from his pockets. Familiar with his body language, we read Thornhill's gesture as a prelude to action.

25. Long shot as in 24. The car continues to approach. It is a black four-door Cadillac, a *film noir* car. Like the sinister sedans of *Out of the Past* and *The Big Sleep*, it threatens to deliver violence and chaos. But it doesn't. It rushes past, and the camera pans again to follow it out of the frame (a simple drive-by shooting, we realize in retrospect, actually would have been an effective way to eliminate Thornhill). Even though we cannot see inside, we assume the Cadillac contains neither a spy nor a rich gangster but ironically just another affluent business professional like Thornhill.

26-31. Mediums shots of Thornhill standing at the roadside followed by POV long shots. The camera set-up remains the same for each medium shot as well as for each long shot. When the Cadillac passes, Thornhill slouches and slides his hands back into his pockets. As the waiting and the false starts continue, we share Thornhill's impatience and frustration (toward Hitchcock the manipulator also). Thornhill begins to frown. Finally, another vehicle approaches from where the Cadillac disappeared.

32. POV long shot. The vehicle comes closer to Thornhill. It is a truck and we hear its distinct motor.

33. Medium shot. Thornhill tenses and glances slightly upward, altering the sight line, signaling a possible break in routine and preparing us for surprises from above.

34. Long shot. Keeping with the pattern, we expect a cut to Thornhill's POV but instead the next shot is a low angle from the opposite side of the road, looking back across at Thornhill silhouetted against the horizon. Interjecting the first of several comic touches, a huge ten-wheeler truck zooms into frame right engulfing Thornhill in a cloud of dust, cartoon-style, the way Road Runner might overwhelm Wile E. Coyote with one of his desert whirlwinds.

35. Medium shot as in 33. In a slow burn as the cloud settles, Thornhill silently wipes a speck of dust from his eye like Oliver Hardy removing some comic debris from his face and clothing. In addition, the progressive physical dismantling of Thornhill is hereby initiated with the soiling of his suit. Returning his left hand to his pocket (the default position), Thornhill shrugs (again the silent comedian) and looks across the road. He straightens his posture as he notes some movement in the landscape.

36. Long shot. Thornhill's POV. From behind the cornfield, a car emerges and travels on a dirt lane that intersects with a wider unpaved road leading to Highway 41. From this perspective, the various roads seem to connect in a diagonal grid. Having possibly been concealed all this time, the car slowly nears.

37-42. Medium shots of observant Thornhill alternate with POV long shots. We know of course that there is no Kaplan but still this approach is ominous. It may be an assassin arranged by Leonard and Eve. That likelihood fades when we notice that the car is a battered green coupe, not the kind of vehicle someone working for Vandamm would use. Thornhill keeps his hands in his pockets but watches the car intently. With a slight pan in the POV, the car stops by the highway (unlike any of the three previous vehicles) and the passenger door opens. Somebody is about to join Thornhill in a desolate location that doesn't invite casual loitering. Hitchcock simultaneously releases us from tedium and rekindles suspense.

43. Medium shot. Thornhill once again straightens and starts to remove hands from pockets.

44. Long shot. A man gets out of the car and immediately projects contradictory visual cues. First, he is waving goodbye to the driver, the gesture of a friend or relative but probably not of one Vandamm thug to another. Next, we notice that he is wearing a brown suit and hat; the color connects him to the drab earth tones of the local landscape and the hat relegates him to the ranks of secondary players (only Licht has worn a hat so far). Finally, he has been deposited by the side of Highway 41 with no luggage of any kind and is presumably not waiting for the Chicago-bound

Greyhound to appear. Something uncertain and unexplainable, therefore, still accrues to his presence.

45. Medium shot. Braced for action, Thornhill completely takes his hands out of his pockets.

46. Long shot. The car turns around and drives off toward the cornfield, drawing our attention once again to what lies beyond the field and outside the frame. The man continues walking forward.

47. Medium close-up. Significantly, Hitchcock moves in closer on Thornhill as another way to build tension regarding the newcomer.

48. Long shot as in 46. The camera pans as the man comes to a stop beside the highway. He stands, like Thornhill, with his hands in his hip pockets and looks to the right, away from the camera. Then, he turns and stares directly at Thornhill, allowing us to read his features. We may not know Malcolm Atterbury's name but we recognize his face. A hotel clerk in *From Here to Texas*. Officer Spitz in *Crime of Passion*. Reverend Hastings in *Stranger at My Door*. All of them, low echelon representatives of order and propriety. This man, we tell ourselves, will not be a threat.

49. Medium close-up. Thornhill leans forward. Hitchcock and Grant keep expanding the physical gesturality even working in this close.

50. Long shot. From ground level, the camera shows Thornhill and the man standing on opposite sides of the highway, starkly backgrounded by the cloudless sky and flat horizon. Longer than any shot since the opening one, it is held for about seven seconds, a tableau vivant resonant of every cultural divide separating America — blue state confronting red, urban prince meeting rural everyman, ad executive encountering consumer.

51. Medium close-up. Thornhill unbuttons his coat (which of course was fashionably correct in being clasped by the top button only), spreads it open and places his hands on his hips. He chews slightly on his lower lip and stares intently across at the man. All the gestures signal puzzled contemplation.

52. Long shot as in 48. The man returns Thornhill's gaze, indicating equal capability and agency on his part.

53. Medium shot. At about ten seconds, another comparatively long held shot containing some detailed physical blocking. Thornhill first looks up the road to see if anything is approaching and then turns back, removing one hand from his hip and staring again at the man. With both hands now lowered to his side, Thornhill starts to cross the highway, the camera panning to keep him in the center of the frame. Taking initiative, Thornhill adopts the role of investigator.

54. Long shot from Thornhill's POV. Hitchcock's trademark subjective camera tracks forward as Thornhill walks across the road. Usually reserved for one character's intrusion into the private space of another, the forward track often ends badly (for example, Martin Balsam's climb up the staircase of the Bates house in *Psycho*). Hands in hip pockets, the man remains completely immobile, staring directly into the camera and keeping us ill at ease.

55. Medium shot. The camera tracks laterally with Thornhill as he continues to traverse the highway. Thornhill's failure to speak or gesture to the man strikes us as a bit unusual. "Why did the silent ad man cross the road?" we ask in a reworking of the classic children's joke.

56. Long shot as in 54. The subjective forward track draws nearer to the man. Even though the camera movement here is not immediately preceded (as usual in Hitchcock and in classic Hollywood cinema) by a shot of Thornhill looking into the camera, we understand the convention and know that this is still Thornhill's POV.

57. Medium shot as in 55. Thornhill stops and the camera continues tracking to bring the man into the frame for a two-shot. Clasping his always restless hands in front of his body and playing with his little finger, Thornhill nods in greeting. The man initially does not respond and, famed Midwestern reticence notwithstanding, we are thrown off by the rudeness. Finally, nearly four minutes into Prairie Stop, Thornhill delivers the first line of dialogue with "hi" followed by the rubbing together of his hands and the comment "hot day."

With no inflection to indicate attitude, the man evenly replies, "Seen worse." Following an uncomfortable silence, Thornhill asks, "Are you supposed to be meeting someone here?" Just in case we might still be mistaking him for one of Vandamm's foreign accented henchmen, the man drops his "g" and answers, "Waitin' for the bus," a fact which he then confirms by looking down the highway to the right and adding "Due any minute." Disappointed, Thornhill can only say, "Oh." Then, in another telegraphing of a plot point that will soon grow ominous, the man looks beyond Thornhill's shoulder toward the opposite side of the road and observes, "Some of them crop-duster pilots get rich…"

58. Long shot from man's POV. We are looking at an empty field and at the small plane on the horizon that we saw earlier. The plane's engine can just barely be heard. Completing the sentence above, the man's off-screen voice offers, "…if they live long enough." With that single reference, the comic overtones of the conversation begin to veer off in a more chilling direction.

59. Medium shot as in 57. Thornhill rubs his hands together again; both men look at the plane and Thornhill softly remarks, "Yeah." Hitchcock, like Shakespeare, has privileged us with information that allows us to appreciate dramatic irony, but still we wonder why Thornhill, turning from the plane to the man, would even ask, "Then,…then your name isn't Kaplan?" Continuing to watch the plane, the man answers, "Can't say it is, 'cause it ain't." As hayseed funnyman, he reasserts a comic touch and leaves us even more confused as to where this encounter is headed. When the sound of another motor overlaps the plane's engine, the man looks down the highway to his right and announces, "Here she comes, right on time," the feminine colloquialism reconfirming his status as a local authority.

60. Long shot from man's POV. A bus approaches; we are unable to determine if it is another Greyhound.

61. Medium shot as in 59. We are not finished with the plane, and the man looks back at it once again. "That's funny," he notes, as in "peculiar" not "humorous," underscoring our perceptual uncertainty as to whether this interaction is intended strictly for

laughs. "What?" responds Thornhill, still playing straightman to the jokester. But then, like some dustbowl Laocoön sensing the strangeness of a big wooden horse, the man cautions, "That plane's dustin' crops where there ain't no crops."

62. Long shot as in 58. In confirmation, we see the plane flying low over the field. Importantly, however, the plane is still lateral to Thornhill and presumably involved in a separate sphere of action.

63. Medium shot. Thornhill and the man stand together at the right side of the frame, Thornhill glancing at the plane and the man watching the slowing bus. The typically balanced center foreground two-shot is disrupted by the persistent encroachment of the plane.

64. Long shot as in 60. The bus comes to a stop close to the camera and looms large in the frame. The diagonal composition and attention to off-screen space (part of the bus already exits lower frame right) are anything but static. There is a gathering momentum, a sense of unstable but certain energy at work within and between the shots.

65. Medium shot as in 63. The door of the bus (a weathered local and not the more deluxe Greyhound) automatically swings open and the man boards. The door closes on Thornhill in a subtle reprise of Hitchcock's opening cameo appearance. The bus recedes into upper frame right as Thornhill stands at the edge of the highway and places his hands on his hips in that familiar sign of indecision and concern. Remembering Eve's instruction that Kaplan would "be there at three-thirty," Thornhill checks his watch, calling our attention to time and to shot duration, which, at over twenty seconds, draws out the anxiety. Finally, Thornhill returns his hands to his hips and looks across the road. Disappearing from sight, the bus briefly leaves Thornhill vulnerable and alone again in the frame.

66. Long shot as in 62. Significantly and ominously, the plane continues to the end of the frame, banks right and flies toward Thornhill, collapsing the division between the two separate zones of action. The previously shared POV shot has now become uniquely Thornhill's.

67. Medium shot. A new camera set-up provides this frontal view of Thornhill with the dirt road and highway marker behind him. He is clasping his hands in front of his body and squinting slightly toward the plane. The plane's engine increases somewhat in volume and broadcasts its closer approach.

68. Long shot from Thornhill's POV. Roughly matching Thornhill's head and eye movements, the camera slightly tilts and pans to follow the plane which has leveled off and is flying straight toward where Thornhill stands at the side of the road. The engine sound links the previous shot and grows louder.

69. Medium shot as in 67. Thornhill is now fully focused on the plane, his eyes registering intense interest.

70. Long shot as in 68. The plane comes closer, descending toward the camera. We can clearly confirm that it is a biplane used for agricultural spraying but also imbued with the martial overtones of a World War I fighter.

71. Medium close-up. The camera has moved in closer to register Thornhill's anxiety. He straightens and brings his arms down to his side, ready to react.

72. Long shot as in 70. The plane now actually dives at the camera, its hostile intent totally clear and its engine overwhelming the soundtrack. Its shape fills the middle of the frame.

73. Close-up. Shaken and afraid, Thornhill ducks and falls out of the bottom of the frame.

74. Medium shot. In a ground-level process shot, Thornhill drops to the dirt, both arms braced in front of him as he lies on his stomach. The plane buzzes Thornhill, almost clipping his head and showering him with dust. After the plane passes, he rises slightly and watches the continuing flight path. For a moment, we think the attack may have ended.

75. Long shot from Thornhill's POV. The plane flies low to the ground, climbs and banks for a turn. We are not certain yet where the plane is headed.

76. Long shot. Thornhill gets up on one knee like a field athlete waiting for the next play. He looks toward the plane.

77. Long shot from Thornhill's POV. The plane circles for another pass; clearly the attack has not ended.

78. Long shot as in 76. Thornhill is all the way up on his feet now with his eyes fixed to the plane's movement.

79. Long shot as in 77. Completing its turn, the plane levels off and begins another attack. Each shot (75-79) in this cross-cutting is held only for about two seconds so that again the editing builds tension.

80. Medium shot. The low angle here immediately signals that Thornhill will be taking to cover. In yet one more variation in the intricately detailed physical blocking Hitchcock has choreographed, Thornhill crouches and turns slightly to the right as if awaiting a starter's gun.

81. Long shot as in 79. The plane dives directly at the camera, assaulting us full on the way the fist-to-camera shots do elsewhere in the film.

82. Medium shot as in 80. Almost like dodging opponents midfield, Thornhill spins to the left and plunges head first toward a ditch beside the road. The camera pans with the dive, which resembles a soldier's leap into a foxhole and sustains the military imagery of the biplane itself.

83. Medium shot. A reverse angle process shot from ground level. The plane zooms in low and strafes the ground with machine-gun bullets. Curiously, some critics have written that the plane attack occurs absent gunfire but the percussive sound and the cartridge detonations are evident both here and in a later shot as well. The humor of the bus interlude recedes now as we realize

that Thornhill's life is in real danger. While annoying, the plane itself will not kill him; the machine gun is necessary to elevate the menace that Hitchcock has been suggesting. With wind and dust swirling around him, Thornhill raises his head to track the course of the plane.

84. Long shot from Thornhill's POV. Again the plane banks in preparation for another pass. The camera pans to follow it.

85. Medium shot as in 83. Thornhill remains in the ditch and comes up on his left arm to continue watching the plane. From the knees up, his body fills the frame and he faces the camera directly, laid out on display for us to best observe his helplessness and despair. The plane can be heard receding and turning in the distance. Thornhill looks behind him down the road, cueing us for the reaction shot which might offer him some assistance.

86. Long shot. Ground level POV. As we hoped, a car is approaching from frame right.

87. Medium shot as in 85. Responding to the car, Thornhill jumps to his feet.

88. Long shot. With a cut on movement that takes us away from the process shot, Thornhill runs to the road, waving his arms and attempting to stop the car. Counting the buses, this is only the sixth vehicle to pass in several minutes and we know that Thornhill must make the best of his opportunity.

89. Medium shot. But the car speeds past and Thornhill stands with his back to the camera watching it go. He is angled slightly to the left. We hear him sigh and imagine the disappointment and panic registering on his face. He looks across the highway at the plane.

90. Long shot. Thornhill's POV. The plane is in the upper left corner of the frame and positioned for another dive.

91. Medium shot. And so begins one of the most famous "pursued man" moments in film history. With no process shot nor special effects, the camera peers over Thornhill's shoulder at the approaching plane. Thornhill watches, turns around toward the viewer searching for a place to hide, looks back at the plane, then swings around again and sprints down the dirt road which intersects the highway. The staging is masterfully precise. Three separate movements are orchestrated and aligned: the biplane coming in low behind Thornhill; Thornhill running and turning around twice to watch the plane gaining on him; the camera reverse tracking out in front of Thornhill as he flees. And all three movements are hurtling toward the viewer and coinciding in that iconic screen image of Cary Grant (not a double and not rear projection) running at the camera while the plane zeroes in over his right shoulder — an image reproduced in posters, advertising and film histories and even meticulously restaged by *Vanity Fair* for its March, 2008, Hollywood issue with Seth Rogen in the Thornhill role (shot not in Bakersfield as the original was but in Camarillo). Finally, at a little over the thirteen second mark, Thornhill dives again for the ground and the plane passes over. (The French title for *North by Northwest*, *La Mort aux Trousses*, translates literally as "Death on the Heels" and stems from this specific image of the lethal plane pursuing Thornhill.)

92. Medium shot. Another cut on movement to a ground level process shot. Thornhill dives head forward onto the dirt road where a second burst of machine-gun fire kicks up dust. Falling to his side in a lateral view, Thornhill arcs his left leg up into the air, striking an athletic dance pose, like Kelly in "Slaughter on Tenth Avenue" or Astaire in "The Girl Hunt Ballet." Looking up at the plane as it passes, Thornhill glances off screen to the right.

93. Long shot at ground level from Thornhill's POV. We know the drill — this shot will identify another course of action for Thornhill to pursue, another Lewis Carroll option to take. Thornhill again spies the dry cornfield which lined the periphery of earlier shots.

94. Medium shot as in 92. Looking at the plane and then at the cornfield as if to weigh his choices, the dancer jumps up.

91. The most famous "pursued man" shot in cinema history.

95. Long shot. Continuing the movement, Thornhill (in a low angle) gets to his feet and runs to the right. In the distance, we see the circling plane.

96. Medium shot. The camera tracks laterally alongside Thornhill while he bolts for the cornfield.

97. Long shot. The camera shoots from behind as Thornhill crosses a strip of bare earth and springs into the cornfield, disappearing behind the parched stalks and tassels. Appropriately, Thornhill will get inside before the camera; we will continue to follow his lead in this chase.

98. Medium shot. The camera looks across the top of the cornfield; the rustling of the stalks indicates Thornhill's movements. His imprint is the kind an animal would make.

99. Medium close-up (studio interior). Hitchcock's transitions from location to studio are sometimes jarring but this one works smoothly primarily because there is no need for a sky and backdrop match. The entire frame is filled with realistic-looking cornstalks. The camera follows Thornhill as he drops to the ground, where, like the animal hinted at in 98, he crouches on all fours. Twice he looks up to check for the plane and then back to the ground. A dried stalk of corn falls to the side. Off-screen, the increasingly loud roar of the plane lets us know that the hunt has not ended.

100. Long shot. A slightly upward tilted camera is positioned just outside the cornfield with a row of stalks stretching beyond the right edge of the frame. The plane approaches from the left and swoops down low over the stalks.

101. Medium close-up as in 99. Thornhill ducks and the stalks rustle when the plane passes overhead, the object defined through its consequence. Thornhill looks up and smiles, cartoon style again, thinking he has eluded his attacker(s). Off-screen, we can hear the sound of the plane coming in close again for another dive. Thornhill's smile wanes, capping off the cartoon reference.

102. Long shot as in 100. The plane maneuvers into a descent.

103. Medium close-up as in 101. Raising himself and looking around, Thornhill worriedly listens to the approaching sound of the engine. Hitchcock's manipulation of screen time continues to be subtly effective. What appeared at first to be an Aristotelian alignment of screen time with real time has actually been either an extension (the cross-cutting as Thornhill watched the cars approach or when he greeted the waiting bus passenger) or a contraction (as is the case here with the amount of time it would physically have taken the plane to complete one pass, straighten out, bank and line up for a second approach).

104. Long shot as in 102. The plane dives at the camera, releasing a cloud of smoke over the cornfield in an aerial chemical attack that prefigures later films like *Goldfinger* and *The Satan Bug*. We are not certain if the gas is crop pesticide or something more immediately lethal.

105. Medium close-up as in 103. Thornhill raises his arm to protect against the white smoke which completely fills the frame and which creates a claustrophobic effect in stark contrast to the intimidating vastness of the opening shots. Over the obscured screen we hear the sound of the plane and of Thornhill's coughing. The smoke clears slowly (running time of the shot is nearly thirteen seconds) and Thornhill is seen using a handkerchief to protect his nose and eyes. The camera follows his movements as he raises himself up and down and then pushes further into the cornfield to avoid the smoke.

106. Long shot. In a transition to a new studio set-up, Thornhill emerges from the cloudy part of the cornfield and runs through the stalks directly toward the camera. Stopping in a low angle close-up, he parts the corn and looks out at the road. His clothes are covered with chemical residue; the publication three years later of Rachel Carson's *Silent Spring* will make his subsequent efforts back in Chicago to have the suit "sponged" clean seem almost pathetically naïve.

107. Long shot from Thornhill's POV. Through the parted corn, a truck can be seen approaching in the distance. There is a deceptively serene painterly quality, like an illustrated candy sampler box, to the way the cornstalks frame the sides of the image.

108. Close-up as in 106. The last of the studio shots. Standing all the way up, Thornhill looks over his shoulder toward the plane and then determinedly back at the road. Acting on the choice we know he will make, Thornhill dashes from the left side of the frame, briefly leaving the camera and the viewer in empty space.

109. Long shot. A reverse angle from the edge of the exterior location's cornfield shows Thornhill (back to camera) running toward the road. The sound of the truck comes closer. We are anxious to see what kind of emotions are registering on Thornhill's face.

110. Long shot. The plane banks and turns while off-screen we hear the truck's horn sounding. Another timed opposition has been launched — Thornhill's race to the truck versus the plane's ongoing assault.

111. Long shot. In a low angle with his back still to the camera, Thornhill darts to the middle of the highway, where he stops and begins to wave his arms wildly at the approaching truck. Among the various tensions here is our still-denied need to see Thornhill's expression.

112. Long shot as in 110. Continuing its turn, the plane prepares for yet one more strike.

113. Medium close-up. We finally see Thornhill's face, and he looks very frightened. In what appears to be rear projection (not always this good in some Hitchcock films), Thornhill glances over his right shoulder at the plane and then with one hand continues to flag down the truck, whose horn, motor and brakes we hear off-screen.

114. Long shot from Thornhill's POV. The truck approaches head-on and continues to sound its horn. It is an oil tanker and a potentially uncontrollable threat (cf. *Terminator 3* and *Casino Royale*).

115. Medium close-up as in 113. Looking at the plane, Thornhill now puts up both hands in a more desperate "stop" signal and bites his lip. The horn sounds continuously. As we might expect, Hitchcock uses cross-cutting between short shots (two seconds on average) to build toward the climax.

116. Long shot as in 114. The truck barrels down on the camera. When it enters medium close-up range, we hear grinding brakes and skidding tires.

117. Medium close-up as in 115. Conveying his fear through facial expression, Thornhill opens his mouth and widens his eyes. He continues to stand firm and to signal. The sound of horn, brakes and tires links this series of shots.

118. Medium close-up as reached in 116. Unable to halt its high speed, the truck rushes into close-up, its front grille completely filling the frame. The mechanical might bearing down on Thornhill seems overwhelming. The horn is even louder.

119. Close-up. Thornhill's face flinches as he prepares for impact. To simulate the forward thrust of the truck, the camera zooms into extreme close-up and Thornhill lifts both hands to protect his face. Accompanied by the sound of the blaring horn, Thornhill's head falls backward.

120. Medium shot. Cut on movement to a low level shot from behind Thornhill as the truck skids forward and knocks him to the highway. The truck's front bumper extends over Thornhill's lower body; we see clearly that this is still Cary Grant doing the stunt and not a double.

121. Medium close-up. A side view showing Thornhill's head hitting the asphalt (the falling motion has linked shots 119-121). Cary Grant lies under the front axle of the now stopped truck and raises his head to look anxiously toward the incoming plane.

122. Long shot from Thornhill's POV. With a truck tire framing the left side of the frame (to heighten Thornhill's claustrophobic entrapment), the plane comes straight toward the truck and the camera. The plane is wobbling as if the pilot has lost control or has shifted into some kind of crazed kamikaze mode.

123. Long shot. A reverse angle from across the highway shows the plane crashing into the second of the two tank trailers. Neither a model nor a process shot, the stunt flying simultaneously immerses us in the realism and prompts us to speculate on the staging.

124. Long shot. And so the climax arrives; the tank explodes and the plane bursts into flame. For the first time in the entire Prairie Stop sequence, as if to emphasize the climax, nondiegetic music, the fandango theme, begins on the soundtrack. The camera is still on the opposite side of the road, closer and at a slightly different angle.

125. Long shot. From ground level, the camera shoots toward the front of the truck and the burning plane. Thornhill (a double this time for Grant) pulls himself out from under the front wheels, his back to the camera. Two men jump from the cab of the truck and one of them shouts to Thornhill, "Get out of here. The other tank may blow." (The first spoken words since the waiting passenger departed on the local bus nearly four minutes earlier.) A logo on the door of the truck identifies the company as Magnum Oil (a client of Thornhill's advertising firm?). The two drivers scramble off to the right while the stunt double backs slowly away from the crash site and watches the conflagration. Thornhill probably still wants to see into the cockpit to determine who has been trying to kill him. Lehman's original script identifies two assassins killed in the crash, Licht being one of them. Hitchcock, however, maintains a dreamlike vagueness and does not show us anyone in the plane.

126. Long shot. Seen from behind, the drivers continue running right toward the cornfield.

127. Medium shot. In a set-up that has now become the standard template for action film explosions (especially the *Mission Impossible* franchise), the camera tracks back from Thornhill as he hurries away from the truck and looks over his shoulder. Upon the detonation of the remaining oil tanker, Thornhill ducks slightly and runs more quickly toward the camera.

128. Medium shot. Reverse angle of Thornhill backing away from the camera (face toward us) and moving into long shot. A significant amount of action occurs in this 10 second shot. A passing car stops at the side of the road and then a battered pickup with a standing refrigerator in the truck bed pulls in front of it — a fleet of vehicles compared to the sporadic passings that Thornhill encountered earlier. A farmer (identified by the denim and straw hat) jumps out of the truck, and two men and a woman (dressed in country not city clothing) get out of the car. "What happened?" the farmer asks Thornhill, who rubs his forehead and gestures toward the flames. We are unable to hear his exact words — having seen the entire incident, we have no need of a superfluous explanation.

129. Long shot. A low angle view of the carnage with the farmer's arm framing the right foreground of the screen. His sleeve is rolled up as if he is prepared to assist somehow.

130. Long shot. In a lateral low angle, Thornhill and the four passersby look screen left at the crash. As the four locals move forward, Thornhill drifts backward and unobtrusively exits the right side of the frame, leaving an eerie piece of profile portraiture somewhere between Walker Evans and Norman Rockwell.

131. Long shot. Seen from behind, the farmer and the three car passengers stand and watch the flames burn out of control. Heat keeps them from moving closer; we do not see the truck drivers anywhere nearby. Something prompts the farmer to look over his shoulder.

132. Long shot. In the reaction shot we anticipate, the pickup truck pulls away from the edge of the road, makes a u-turn and speeds off in the direction of Chicago.

133. Long shot as in 131. Completing his pivot, the farmer waves his arms, runs toward the camera and chases after his truck. "Hey," he shouts, astonished at this breakdown in rural order.

134. Long shot as in 132. A comic denouement as the farmer runs down the highway, Keystone Kops style, waving his arms and yelling, "Come back! Hey! Come back." Deflated, the farmer finally stops in the middle of the highway and watches his truck disappear in the distance. The nondiegetic music ends, and instead of a silent film iris-in we have a dissolve to the truck parked along the curb of Michigan Avenue later that evening. Two policemen are examining it carefully, surprised perhaps by the abandoned refrigerator still resting in back.

Thus, we have entered and exited Prairie Stop on a dissolve, appropriate transition for a nightmare. Swinging wildly between comedy and anxiety, exposure and claustrophobia, we have accompanied Roger Thornhill on a journey of extreme sensations. Ernest Lehman drafted the original screenplay to include various helicopter shots of Thornhill being chased by the biplane and running in and out of the cornfield. Except for the opening crane shot, however, Hitchcock has kept us tightly on the ground with Thornhill. From above, we would be observing Thornhill; on the ground we are identifying with him. We have experienced his frustration, his fear and his uncertain relief. We have also experienced a bravura piece of filmmaking, where simultaneously we have appreciated the technique and been manipulated by its effectiveness.

19: "VALUABLE PROPERTY"

The crop-dusting attack and the Mount Rushmore chase are widely admired as *North by Northwest's* most dazzling and technically proficient set pieces. Somewhat less showy but also impressive is the Shaw and Oppenheim auction sequence, notable for its intricate staging and its thematic resonance.

The auction is bookended by two similar long shots, the first of Thornhill arriving by taxi and entering 1212 North Michigan and the final of Thornhill exiting the gallery in police custody and departing in a squad car. At the Shaw and Oppenheim gallery, Thornhill joins a scene *in media res*, a fact which emphasizes that the action once again is beyond his control. Throughout the episode he struggles initially to understand identities and motivations and then just to get away unharmed.

The first words we hear are those of the off-screen auctioneer detailing one of the *objets d'art* up for sale: "…this magnificent pair of Louis Seize fauteuils. Original gilt finish. Upholstered in pure silk damask. How much may I say to start? What am I bid?" The camera opens on a close-up of a man's arm first caressing Eve's bare shoulders and then sliding upward to lightly squeeze her neck. The gesture is proprietary, equating Eve with the fauteuils and the other expensive treasures available to the highest bidder. As the camera pulls further backward, we can identify the man as Vandamm, who casually returns his hand to Eve's shoulder. Accompanying Vandamm is his personal secretary Leonard. Continuing to track backward, the camera reaches long shot distance and then slowly pans across the dense, well-dressed audience, moving past the auctioneer, until it reaches the rear entrance, where Thornhill stands and looks over toward Eve. He frowns and the camera tracks forward to frame him in a medium shot. In this one uninterrupted long take, Hitchcock links Thornhill to Vandamm and Eve in a way that suggests some tense marketplace dispute over ownership rights. During the camera's sweep across the room, the auctioneer has continued to entertain bids: "Four-fifty is bid for the pair. Can I hear five hundred? Will you say five hundred? Can I say the five hundred? Fair warning and last call — sold to Mr. Stone, second row. Four hundred and fifty dollars." In fact, the auctioneering continues as running choral commentary throughout the entire scene, often forcing Vandamm and Thornhill to speak over it. The auctioneer's dialogue is intrusive, a language of commerce in which everyone and everything has exchange value. It reminds us that the main characters are looking to buy not only artifacts but also loyalty, approval, government secrets and time.

Thornhill's jealousy makes him aggressive. Seeing Eve with Vandamm, he strides determinedly across the room, the camera tracking along with him, first backward and then forward, as if following an infantry charge. Striking the first blow in the verbal badinage to follow, Thornhill makes his comment comparing the couple and Leonard to a portrait by Charles Addams and Vandamm counters by asking Thornhill what "possessed" him "to come blundering in here like this." During the interchange, the auctioneer continues to take bids on a "lovely Aubusson settee" which ultimately goes for a thousand dollars and is the second piece of auctioned furniture to remind Thornhill how much he'd probably like to sit down and rest. Hitchcock's staging here is brilliant. Eve is seated facing out at the viewer; Vandamm is standing to her left and Leonard is lounging against a table somewhat to Vandamm's left and is turned partially toward Vandamm and away from the viewer. Thornhill is behind Eve's right shoulder. Hitchcock cross-cuts between this composition and another four-shot in which the camera is just behind Thornhill's right shoulder looking across at Eve in profile and at both Vandamm and Leonard slightly turned to look at Thornhill. In both cases we are able to see the effect Thornhill's words have on Eve but he is not.

Like some jilted schoolboy, Thornhill insults Eve relentlessly. When Leonard suspiciously questions whether he has been in Eve's hotel room, Thornhill replies, "Sure, isn't everybody?" Beginning now to doubt her loyalty, Vandamm removes his hand from Eve's shoulder and we see her eyes shift nervously in response. Hearing the bids swirl around him, Thornhill says, "I'll bet you paid plenty for this little piece of sculpture." Eve looks straight ahead in discomfort and Vandamm grimly studies her reaction. Continuing his resentful comparison of Eve to an expensive ornament, Thornhill says, "She's worth every dollar of it, take it from me. She puts her heart into her work. In fact her whole body." Meanwhile Vandamm (usually, as at the Townsend mansion, a much better multi-tasker) is suffering from polyphonic overload. He is trying simultaneously to spar with

Thornhill, keep track of the bidding on the pre-Columbian statuette he wants and monitor Eve's body language. Annoyed, he mocks Thornhill for playing "the peevish lover stung by jealousy and betrayal." Hitchcock cuts into the master shot with several close-ups and medium shots; in three of them, the Professor appears just barely visible in the lower left edge of the frame as a member of the audience. How appropriate that

Thornhill and Vandamm compete for "possession" of Eve Kendall as she is seated among other valuable auction items.

the first time all the major characters come together it is for a scene both literally and figuratively devoted to the notions of competition and trade.

Continuing to critique Thornhill's various performances, Vandamm warns that Thornhill's "next role" in which he will be "quite convincing" is the one where he will "play dead." Still obsessed with Eve, Thornhill asks whether he is going to be "dropped into a vat of molten steel and become part of a new skyscraper" or whether "this female" is going "to kiss me again and poison me to death." The characters form an inverted triangle with Thornhill on screen left, Eve in the center and Vandamm on screen right in one of those heavily symbolic compositions, like Melanie Daniels photographed among expensive caged birds, that Hitchcock uses to objectify the female as decorative and exotic. In this case, Eve is seated in her red and black brocaded evening gown against a background of gilded urns and curios looking out at the audience while Thornhill and Vandamm are turned toward each other, two alpha males battling over a prized possession. When Thornhill refers to the poisoned kiss (a reversal of the usual life-restoring kiss of fairy tales), Eve jumps from her seat to strike him with her purse (the same heavily coded accessory that Melanie, in a similar loss of power, continually leaves behind her in *The Birds*). "Who are you kidding? You have no feelings to hurt," Thornhill tells Eve as he blocks her arm and she returns to her seat, resigned to the role of passive albeit now devalued trophy.

Concluding that he may be better off with the police, Thornhill prepares to make a dramatic exit. "Good night, sweetheart," he tells Eve. "Don't think it wasn't nice." Again, we can see the reaction still denied Thornhill; Eve's eyes fill with tears, and immediately we forgive her for the whole crop-dusting incident. Successive tracking shots accompany Thornhill's walk down the aisle. One of them, a forward track from Thornhill's point of view, registers the shock of seeing Leonard materialize from behind a curtain to block the stage exit. Valerian already has positioned himself in front of the rear exit. With his escape routes cut off, Thornhill looks around and pushes onto an aisle seat, forcing two women to scrunch together on their folding chairs.

Hitchcock now goes to work orchestrating multiple actions in one of his trademark crowd scenes. The auctioneer starts the bidding on an early seventeenth-century painting, and Vandamm hurriedly leaves the gallery with Eve. Moving from an opening bid of a thousand dollars to twenty-two fifty, the painting gets a last call when Thornhill suddenly interrupts first with a bid of fifteen hundred followed by an even lower one of twelve hundred. When it is sold at its last highest bid, Thornhill shouts, "Twenty-two fifty? For that chromo?" disrupting public decorum in the same way Grant as Sergeant Cutter breaks into song to interrupt the Thuggee cult gathering in *Gunga Din*. (Thornhill's word choice is revealing; "chromo" is probably short for "chromolithograph," a multicolor commercial print sometimes used for calendar art and advertising, media with which ad man Thornhill would be professionally familiar. The implied criticism touches upon his own self image.) In an attempt to restore order, the auctioneer proceeds to item one hundred ten in the catalogue, announcing it as a "Louis Quinze carved and gilded..." before Hitchcock muffles the exact nomenclature just as he did with the painting so that the references to selling remain broad and all-inclusive. Like a lounge heckler who won't go away, Thornhill shouts, "How do we know it's not a fake? It looks like a fake." Whirling around in an agitated state, a society matron sneers, "Well one thing we know. You're no fake. You're a genuine idiot."

Thornhill's rude commentary and continued inappropriate bidding draw a series of rapidly edited reaction shots. From Thornhill's farewell rejection of Eve to his exit from the gallery, there are a little over seventy shots, all of them showing Thornhill's behavior or the effect of that behavior on others. The auctioneer and his assistant struggle to remember bids, Leonard looks alarmed, Valerian frowns in frustration, several audience members laugh and a battery of old white men turn their angry faces toward Thornhill, who suddenly looks even more tanned and "other" in this sea of wealthy Anglo-Saxon outrage. (Hitchcock, the son of a greengrocer, reveals his residual class resentment as he uses point of view shots to strengthen our allegiance to Thornhill as he confronts the George Grosz-like bourgeoisie.) Finally a pair of uniformed policemen appears, and Thornhill makes sure he gets arrested by starting a fight with a gallery employee. As Thornhill is taken away, the camera pans past a phone booth, and we see the Professor about to call the policemen's superiors.

Almost ten minutes have passed since Thornhill's arrival at the auction, enough time for six separate items, including the Tarascan statuette, to be sold. Real time and screen time have coincided. Thornhill's final comment, delivered to Sergeant Flamm and his partner as they place him in their squad car, indicates that he is beginning to understand his own role in a world where everything, including people's loyalties and destinies, is up for sale. "Handle with care, fellas!" he tells them. "I'm valuable property!"

20: "THE MAN ON LINCOLN'S NOSE"

Looking at the Mount Rushmore monument and reading it like a piece of text, you start with Washington on the left, the tallest and most fully developed of the four Presidential heads. Along with a broad, high-foreheaded face, there are sloping shoulders and a slightly skewed collar. His gaze is direct and turned a few degrees left. Next to Washington, further to the right and lower, is Jefferson, who looks out in the opposite direction. His eyes are the most expressive and fully realized. Teddy Roosevelt is just down from Jefferson, and the top of his head levels off at the monument's lowest elevation. Like Jefferson, Roosevelt gazes to the right; a heavy brow tends to obscure his eyes. Across from Roosevelt and somewhat separated from the first three equally distanced heads is Lincoln. His chin dips below Roosevelt's, but his hair reaches a bit higher. Lincoln's head and eye line are turned sharply back to the left, gazing across and beyond Washington.

Hitchcock is careful to give us several long-held establishing shots of Mount Rushmore. The monument hovers like an *idée fixe* over multiple scenes before the chase itself even begins. In a complicated shot packed with narrative significance, Thornhill stands on the Chicago tarmac and learns from the Professor (who has been pressuring him to continue impersonating Kaplan in Rapid City) that he has probably put double agent Eve Kendall's life in danger. The camera tracks in for a close-up; Thornhill looks stricken as light from a passing plane flickers across his face. By means of a dissolve, his face is superimposed over the Mount Rushmore heads. Once Thornhill's face fades, the monument long shot holds for several seconds until it zooms forward and irises in, revealing itself to be a point of view as Thornhill looks through a tourist telescope at the carvings. Immediately we realize that Thornhill has acceded to the Professor's request and that Mount Rushmore, which the Professor has already identified as Vandamm's "jumping off point to leave the country," is going to figure significantly in some climactic action. The Presidential heads loom behind the Professor as he talks with Thornhill on the observation deck and again most dramatically in the two-shot where the Professor promises Thornhill that "after tonight" his "blessings" will be on both Thornhill and Eve. When all of the major players gather in the cafeteria, the monument fills the background just as it does when Eve makes her escape in the convertible and Roger is loaded into the park ranger station wagon. It is there again in the upper right corner of the frame for Roger and Eve's Black Forest rendezvous and in the upper left corner for Thornhill's nighttime arrival by taxi at Vandamm's hideaway.

The monument's visual prominence is important because once the chase begins, our spatial orientation is a lot shakier. Thornhill and Eve climb down Mount Rushmore between Washington and Jefferson, Valerian comes down on the left side of Washington and Leonard descends a sheer cliff to the right of Lincoln. After they all reach chin level, Leonard starts to move screen left underneath Lincoln then Roosevelt and then Jefferson. At first Thornhill and Eve run to the right but when Thornhill sees Leonard closing in, they turn and climb up over rocks toward the left. That is where they are ambushed by Valerian, who has inched around from the far side of Washington. Thornhill's struggles with first Valerian and then Leonard both occur at the base of Washington's head. None of this, however, is clear in a first or even second viewing of the film. For typical audiences, it is all just a quickly edited tangle of characters sliding down cliffs and clambering over ledges, a glimpse of Roosevelt's eye or Jefferson's nose or Lincoln's beard appearing and disappearing in the background. Confusion is Hitchcock's desired intent. Suspense and disorientation work together; the viewer is never sure exactly where the camera is, how close Thornhill and Eve are to their assailants and from behind which Presidential profile Valerian or Leonard may lunge. The space is cramped and there is little room for maneuverability.

The sense of claustrophobia is just one of the many ways in which Mount Rushmore differs from Prairie Stop. The two sequences, in fact, constitute bookended set pieces. Where Prairie Stop is flat and expansive, Mount Rushmore is steep and confined. Prairie Stop's danger plays out in glaring daylight; Mount Rushmore's comes at night. Silence is crucial to how the crop-dusting scene works; the sound of the attacking biplane pulses slowly to life in the still prairie afternoon and builds relentlessly to an alarming roar. Except for the closing seconds there is no music score at all. By contrast, the chase over the Presidential heads is propelled by the non-stop fandango theme which begins when Eve bolts from the departing airplane and reaches its finale when the Twentieth-Century Limited blasts into its tunnel.

The Mount Rushmore chase is a set piece in the truest, most literal sense of the term, shot as it is almost completely in the studio (another point of comparison with the extensive location shooting of the Prairie

Thornhill and Eve move back toward Washington.

Stop sequence). Denied permission to film close to the monument itself, Hitchcock picked up some interior and exterior shots at the observation center and then retreated to the M-G-M studios. With a team consisting of production designer Robert Boyle, art directors William Horning and Merrill Pye and set decorators Henry Grace and Frank McKelvey, he constructed a massive mock-up of the monument on a sound stage. Given the actual geography of the Borglum sculpture and the physical impossibility, there was never a plan to put real actors on the Presidential heads, but the Department of the Interior also had refused permission even to have figures scrambling over the faces of the reproduced carvings. Quite specifically, the Interior Department officials mandated that the actors could slide down only between the heads and conduct their chase at the shoulders or below the chins. In the end, that's exactly how the sequence was filmed even though the towering background profiles still give us the illusion of Grant and company actually being on the treacherous facial surfaces of the monument.

The Mount Rushmore climax succeeds as well as it does partly because of techniques that old pros like Hitchcock had been utilizing since their silent days. For the scenes of Cary Grant and Eva Marie Saint dangling from cliffs, Hitchcock positioned them horizontally on flat ridged sets and then tilted the camera. When Thornhill looks into the distance and sees a huge Presidential head with Valerian or Leonard climbing alongside it, Hitchcock uses a matte shot to combine either a model or painting with the live action. And in those scenes where Thornhill and Eve are framed on a precipice with the ground and the observatory looming far beneath them, the actors are performing on an angled set in front of a rear projection or a process screen. The look of realism is helped out by the nighttime setting; it is too dark for us to notice problematic stage craft. Similarly, with no single shot in the nearly seven minute, one hundred and some shot montage held for more than a few seconds, we also do not have time to carefully scout out mismatches.

Since he was filming on a carefully controlled sound stage, Hitchcock could have craned his camera extensively in and around the set, showing actors pressed against the facade or peering over the edges. However, not only would lush camera movement foreground the model and emphasize its obvious artifice, so also would it diminish the sense of constricted space. The camera moves very little during the Mount Rushmore chase. The six limited tracking shots are used to accent Roger and Eve's vulnerability or to set up an assault. As they climb down the monument and reach the base of Washington's chin, the camera tracks forward from a long shot to a medium shot, emphasizing their exhaustion, their tenuous toehold on the ridge and the loss of Eve's shoes. Later, tracking laterally, the camera moves left with Thornhill and Eve while they inch across the ledge, their backs to the mountainside. As they advance further and pass a large boulder, the camera tracks quickly backward to reveal Valerian crouched in wait above them and ready to lunge at Thornhill. In the fight that follows, Thornhill shoves Valerian off the mountain but then has to make his way back to Eve, who has been attacked by Leonard and pushed over a cliff. His scramble up the side of the monument is paralleled by a lateral track revealing the difficulty of the terrain. Reaching her and readjusting his grip several times, Thornhill ends up clinging to the edge with one hand, holding Eve with the other and asking Leonard for help. In a stop and start progression, the camera tracks first from medium shot to close-up, showing Thornhill's hand grasping the rock next to Leonard's foot and then into an extreme close-up as Leonard lifts his foot and brings it down on Roger's fingers.

Visually, low-angles and close-ups dominate the Mount Rushmore camera set-ups. The extreme low-angles thrust Thornhill and Eve up against the mountain, the Presidential faces staring down at them in stony disregard. In one such composition, they begin to pick their way down the steep decline separating Washington and Jefferson, and the two heads seem to crush them in the space between. There are at least a dozen low-angle shots throughout the sequence, each one filling the frame and emphasizing the enormity of the surroundings. When Valerian pounces on Thornhill, a low angle shows him commanding the upper half of the screen, and when Eve struggles with Leonard for possession of the statuette, a low angle magnifies his physical advantage over her. In both cases, the camera placement also communicates the "threat from above" motif expressed throughout the film. As mentioned earlier, the close-ups reveal hands and feet fighting for a hold on the mountain. Eve's desperation and physical "dismantling," in particular, progress as she clambers over the rocks. In a series of close-ups, she breaks the heel of a shoe, grabs and rips Roger's hip pocket to stop a fall, abandons her jacket and clings to Roger with one hand as she swings precariously over the heights (much like Katherine Hepburn holding onto Cary Grant as she dangles from the brontosaurus scaffolding in *Bringing Up Baby*). Leonard's ultimate demise is also captured in close-up. His foot fills the screen, mashes Roger's fingers and then, in signature Hitchcock synecdoche, falls out of the right side of the frame upon the off-screen sound of a gunshot.

In *North by Northwest*, Hitchcock caps his career-long interest in using architectural icons to threaten actors. In *The Man Who Knew Too Much* it was Albert Hall; in *Saboteur* it was Radio City Music Hall and the Statue of Liberty; in *Vertigo*, it was all of San Francisco. During his interview with Truffaut, Hitchcock explained that the Mount Rushmore scene provided an opportunity to correct an error he believed that he had made in shooting *Saboteur's* climax on the Statue of Liberty. "If we'd had the hero," said Hitchcock, "instead of the villain hanging in mid-air, the audience's anguish would have been much greater" (p. 106). So to make sure the audience had more emotional investment this time, he substituted hero Robert Cummings trying to save bad guy Otto Kruger with villain Martin Landau trying to send both Eva Marie Saint and Cary Grant into the abyss. The doubled reversal works. In the Truffaut interview, Hitchcock also admits that using Mount Rushmore is something he had "been wanting to do…for years" (p. 108). Ernest Lehman has also noted that "Hitchcock always wanted to do a chase across the faces of Mount Rushmore. You might say it was…a goal we had to get to. Who was getting there, and why, who was chasing whom, and why — that was all a total mystery" (Brady, p. 187). In fact, Lehman even for a while used *The Man on Lincoln's Nose* as a working title for the *North by Northwest* script (a curious choice which would have made *Saboteur's* same mistake of highlighting the villain since it is only Leonard and not Thornhill who ever gets close to Lincoln). The liberties Hitchcock takes in moving characters across the surface of the monument are matched by those in situating Mount Rushmore itself. At work is the kind of creative cartography that designed the Bodega Bay layout in *The Birds*. There is, of course, no ultramodern vacation home adjacent to the monument, no private landing strip concealed by it, no forest pathway that leads to the top of it and no hotel-like observatory directly below it.

For all its physical thrills, the Mount Rushmore chase also accomplishes several important narrative functions, another way in which it differs from the crop-dusting sequence. Both Valerian and Leonard are dispatched (cast into the pit) and Vandamm is apprehended by the Professor and the state troopers. The Professor's rescue of Roger and Eve seals his blessing of the relationship and his release of Eve from government service. The microfilm is retrieved, and state secrets presumably are kept out of the hands of foreign enemies. More importantly, Thornhill proposes to Eve while hanging off the side of the mountain, transcending his self-centeredness in some witty dialogue about how boring his former wives found his life to be. Even the new couple's marriage is accomplished through a "magical" cut that takes them from cliff's edge to Pullman berth. That all of this occurs on a symbolically significant mountain top further magnifies the importance of the sequence, which is given proper literary foreshadowing by having Thornhill scale the rocky exterior of Vandamm's hideaway and Eve ask for her champagne "over the rocks."

After the bravura show-piece that is the Prairie Stop crop-dusting attack, Hitchcock needed a big finish. He got it with the Mount Rushmore chase, an eleven o'clock number if ever there was one. Bringing all his main characters back on stage for some highly polished acrophobic suspense, he built a formula that has been worked even further by *A View to a Kill's* Golden Gate Bridge climax and *Mission Impossible 4's* Burj Khalifa stunt. After *North by Northwest*, Hitchcock did not return to well-known public heights and last-minute chases. The bar had already been set.

21: FANDANGO

Bernard Herrmann composed the scores for eight consecutive Hitchcock films beginning with *The Trouble with Harry*, concluding with *Marnie* and including the electronic soundtrack for *The Birds*. Herrmann also wrote music for *Torn Curtain*, but his collaboration with Hitchcock ended bitterly during production, and the final score was provided instead by John Addison. Each of Herrmann's eight compositions is rich, innovative and uniquely evocative of the specific film for which it was created. To hear the shrieking strings of *Psycho's* shower scene or the muted lyricism of *Vertigo's* "Scene d'Amour" is to immediately experience a Proustian reliving of the one film's blunt horror and the other's romantic dread. As independent pieces, the scores of both *Psycho* and *Vertigo* have been performed by symphony orchestras around the world, and *Vertigo's* music has been borrowed directly for other films (*The Artist*) and for stage productions (*An Inspector Calls*). In recent years, the score for *North by Northwest* has begun to achieve this same respect and admiration and has been included regularly in CD anthologies of classic film scores.

Central to *North by Northwest's* musical structure is the fandango theme. Linked to Spanish folk and flamenco dance, fandango music works on a ¾ pattern that starts out in A minor and progresses to E Major. Its roots are up for debate; perhaps Greek and Roman culture, maybe the West Indies or Latin America. As accompaniment to either solo or couples dancing, the fandango begins slowly and gradually increases in tempo, punctuated by hand-clapping and castanets. Fandango has been referenced in classical works by Scarlatti, Gluck, Mozart and other composers. Herrmann's structural variation is to speed up the tempo, play duple against triple meter and emphasize the brass.

Beginning over the opening credits, the fandango powers the relentless, non-stop chase that is *North by Northwest*. Associated immediately with images of rush hour New Yorkers pouring out of office buildings, it conveys an accelerated urban rhythm that soon transitions into something even more driven, more desperate. As Roger Thornhill is held down and force fed bourbon in the Townsend library, the solemn base chords of the interlude music modulate into the fandango theme, which then accompanies the entire harrying drunk-driving sequence. Various elements combine here to create tension — the rapid cuts, the double exposures from Thornhill's blurry point of view, the murky lighting and of course the pounding fandango. At key points throughout the film, the fandango reappears to quicken the pace and underscore a new iteration of Thornhill's flight, most noticeably when Thornhill pulls the knife from Townsend and escapes the U.N. Building; the tanker truck and plane burst into flames at the end of the crop-dusting sequence; Thornhill navigates an exit from the auction; Thornhill and the Professor hurry on to the Chicago airport tarmac; Thornhill skips out of the Rapid City hospital and scales Vandamm's mountain hideout; and, finally, Eve and Thornhill scramble over Mount Rushmore to elude Vandamm's henchmen. In each instance Thornhill is in motion, pursuing a lead or, more often, evading a threat. Usually, like a fine engine sputtering to life and then advancing smoothly into high gear, a few intermittent low notes ominously signal menace and then build into a forceful, fully orchestrated expression of the fandango chase theme. Referring to the credit sequence use of the theme, Herrmann himself called it a prelude to "the crazy dance about to take place between Cary Grant and the world" (Sullivan, p. 235).

Heard almost as frequently as the fandango is Roger and Eve's love theme. In his book *Hitchcock's Music*, Jack Sullivan calls this piece "Herrmann's most graceful love theme, a languorous oboe-clarinet duet that heats up an already sexy train pickup" (p. 239). Our first encounter with the love theme reveals just how subtly and effectively Hitchcock weaves it into the narrative. After calling Thornhill on his phony "Jack Phillips, western sales manager for Kingby Electronics" identity, Eve hints that "it's going to be a long night" and that she doesn't "particularly like the book" she has started. When she asks Thornhill, "Do you know what I mean?" the diegetic dining car background music ("Fashion Show") fades into nondiegetic train rhythms that then transform into the love theme. Lush and fully developed, the love theme plays all during Eve's cigarette lighting seduction and up through the giving of her sleeping compartment number to Thornhill. It begins again, after Thornhill has been "unpacked" from the berth and the policemen have departed, when Roger and Eve stand before each other and embrace. It is there throughout the famous rotating kiss, pausing abruptly when the porter rings to make up Eve's room. Humorously accenting Thornhill's "Now where were we?" comment, the theme continues when the porter leaves and the lovers coyly banter over the fact that there is only one bed. "You know what that means?" asks Thornhill. "It means you're going to sleep on the floor," replies Eve, and the camera tracks forward to a very tight close-up of the two of them kissing. As Eve glances furtively toward the corridor, where she has just given the porter a note to take to Vandamm, the love theme ends ominously on a sustained somber chord. The music is cuing us to the dangers within this nascent sudden romance.

The love theme is also used ironically to belie what the characters sometimes are saying and doing to each other. Furious at Eve for her apparent betrayal in sending him off to the crop-dusting ambush, Thornhill refuses to touch Eve as she embraces him when he shows up unexpectedly in her Ambassador East Hotel room. The accompanying love theme mocks Eve's behavior at the same time that it reminds us there is still strong mutual attraction here. At this point in the film, Eve is still an enigma; we do not know yet that she is a double agent nor whether her loyalties lie with Vandamm or Thornhill. So when she tells Thornhill to "stay far away from me and don't come near me again," the overlapping love theme is either a bittersweet reminder of cooled passion or an ironic contradiction of Eve's harsh brush-off.

Sullivan identifies as a consistent technique this counterpoint between what often we see on the screen and hear on the soundtrack. "Sometimes the music moves beyond irony to outright deception," he writes, "cuing Hitchcock's preoccupation with doubles and facades in a world where nothing is what it seems. Herrmann delivers his creepiest chords during and following Eve's fake killing of Roger — an insidiously manipulative scene — making us cringe every time we view it, even though we know the trick…music becomes part of an elaborate lie; with chords that deadly, how could the bullets not be real?" (p. 238). Laughter and dread become mixed up in ways that are emphasized by the music. "Three gruff ascending chords" which accompany Thornhill's forced bourbon drinking "become terrifying when transformed into screeching strings at the precipice from which the kidnappers contrive to hurl Grant and his car" (p. 238), yet there is also something comic, almost slapstick, about the entire drunk driving episode as communicated by Cary Grant's mugging and mumbling.

Also significant is the way in which the love theme and fandango intermingle with one another. For example, as Thornhill, in redcap disguise, carries Eve's luggage along the station platform and tells her that she's "the smartest girl" he "ever spent the night with on a train," the love theme strikes up in acknowledgement of their affair. When the policemen discover the old redcap in his underwear, however, the love theme shifts into the fandango and the police burst into the lobby looking for Thornhill. Conversely, the chase music which accompanies Thornhill to the art gallery in pursuit of Eve blends into a dark variation of the love theme once he enters the auction room and sees Eve seated with Vandamm. As a result of the train trip to Chicago, Thornhill's life has become even more complicated. Still evading the authorities and still searching for the nonexistent Kaplan, he is also coping with decidedly mixed feelings for Eve. His emotional turmoil is reflected in Herrmann's fragmented structure — abrupt starts and finishes, a few striking chords to echo a theme, ominous variations and the merging of the fandango and the love theme motifs. The ending provides both narrative and musical resolution. From the pre-boarding rescue of Eve to the climactic shooting of Leonard, the fandango propels the entire Mount Rushmore sequence. At the moment Roger says, "Come along, Mrs. Thornhill" and the cliffside grasp transitions to a lift into the matrimonial sleeping berth, the fandango transforms into the love theme, the finality of which is emphasized by pounding timpani as the train enters its infamous tunnel.

Less "definitive" than the two themes is the brief interlude music which sets tone and links scenes. Abbreviated and usually foreboding, these chords often echo or vary the thematic notes. The interlude music covers movement from one geographical space to another. It accompanies Thornhill as he returns to the Townsend mansion with the detectives, as he leaves the mansion and arrives at the Plaza with his mother, as he and his mother leave the hotel room and enter the elevator and as he rushes into a taxi outside the hotel and arrives at the U.N. Building. Eve's actions also receive distinct musical attention. Sudden suspenseful chords intrude when she observes policemen boarding the train ("They weren't smiling"), speaks to Leonard from the station phone booth, "shoots" Thornhill in the cafeteria and jumps into her white convertible after the Black Hills rendezvous with Thornhill. Similarly ominous music attends the farewell moments at Vandamm's vacation retreat. Leonard's words ("I know how fond you are of Miss Kendall") as well as his actions (picking up Thornhill's matchbook) become especially sinister through Herrmann's cues. And when Vandamm says that Eve's disloyalty will be "best disposed of from a great height" and when he clutches her arm as they walk toward the plane, the violence beneath his suave exterior is made even more palpable by a menacing variation in the music's major themes.

The free-floating nature of the interlude music, argues Sullivan, creates the score's "modernist objectivity" with the "melodies refusing to attach themselves to specific characters or settings" (p. 239). The confusion is intentional; the danger is omnipresent. Sullivan's examples convey his authoritative understanding of Herrmann's design: "The vibraphone chords hovering like a low-grade fever over the elaborate Grand Central

Bernard Herrmann created scores for eight of Hitchcock's most popular films.

phone-booth scene and over the sweeping establishing shot in the auction have little to do with Wagnerian leitmotifs or inner revelations; the mysterious modal chords floating through Lester Townsend's house just before Vandamm goes in to meet his kidnapped victim…are not married to Roger or his nemesis" (pp. 239-40).

Frequently in Hitchcock's films the main character delivers a musical performance. Farley Granger (*Rope*) and Tippi Hedren (*The Birds*) play the piano, Henry Fonda (*The Wrong Man)* strums the bass, Marlene Dietrich (*Stage Fright*) and Doris Day (*The Man Who Knew Too Much*) sing. Cary Grant doesn't really perform musically but he does sing a drunken version of "I've Grown Accustomed to Her Face" and whistles "Singing in the Rain" in Eve's hotel room shower. His knowledge of musicals (remember those Winter Garden Theatre tickets) is part of the film's overall pop culture allusiveness, which surfaces in the diegetic Muzak references as well. When Thornhill first enters the Plaza lobby and walks to the Oak Bar, we can hear the jokingly prescient "It's a Most Unusual Day" from *A Date with Judy* playing in the background. The dining car music which Herrmann uses as a segue into the love theme is André Previn's "Fashion Show." Like the extremely self-referential Hitchcock, Herrmann also borrows from himself. "A quotation from *Vertigo,* the ultimate music of longing," writes Sullivan, "caresses Eve's sultry eyes as she embraces Roger in her hotel following his harrowing encounter with the crop duster" (pp. 238-39). Sullivan also identifies "the Vertigo chord" when the fandango chase transitions into the love theme during the Mount Rushmore climax.

Another Hitchcock and Herrmann trademark at work in *North by Northwest* is the use of prolonged silence for certain key scenes. Except for a rekindled fandango theme during the final seconds, the crop-dusting sequence has no music track at all. In fact, as we have seen, it has only fourteen lines of dialogue. Silence is the whole point here; it emphasizes Thornhill's isolation and vulnerability. As with similar long stretches of silence in *The Birds* and *Marnie*, Hitchcock uses the technique to build suspense, to play out the viewer's wariness over what might come bursting from the edge of the frame to threaten Thornhill. Surfacing from the stillness, the motorized whir of passing cars, the drone of the biplane and the spectacular explosion of the tanker truck become even more abrupt and dangerous. In the airport tarmac scene, Hitchcock again dispenses with music and generates tension around the Professor and Thornhill's efforts to communicate critical information over the roar of multiple airplane engines.

Hitchcock always thought carefully about how music would be used in his films, making detailed and informed planning notes. As important a tool to him as camera movement and editing, the music score helped to create the exact emotional resonance he wanted for a particular scene. Bernard Herrmann seemed to always instinctively understand where Hitchcock was going with his overall concept for a film. Their partnership is one of cinema's great director/composer collaborations, similar to that between Fellini and Nino Rota, Sergio Leone and Ennio Morricone, Blake Edwards and Henry Mancini or Tim Burton and Danny Elfman. Herrmann seems especially suited to Hitchcock's blend of ironic romanticism and existential dread. A *North by Northwest* with, say, Max Steiner would be unthinkable.

22: AUTRE AUTEUR

As Alfred Hitchcock and Ernest Lehman sat around the director's office pitching each other the basic outline of *North by Northwest*, a great deal of Hitchcock, from plot points to character arcs, made it into the finished product. Many signature elements of Lehman's published fiction were blended in as well.

A former copywriter for Broadway press agent Irving Hoffman, Lehman had a long and successful Hollywood career. He wrote the scripts for *Executive Suite, Sabrina, From the Terrace, Somebody Up There Likes Me, The Prize* and *Black Sunday* as well as the screen adaptations of several popular Broadway musicals including *The King and I, West Side Story, The Sound of Music* and *Hello, Dolly*. He also adapted his own novelette *Sweet Smell of Success* for the screen and adapted and produced *Who's Afraid of Virginia Woolf*. For Hitchcock, in addition to *North by Northwest*, he wrote *Family Plot* and *The Short Night*, which was planned but never filmed.

Along with the novelettes *Sweet Smell of Success* and *The Comedian* (which Lehman adapted for television), Lehman wrote two novels (*The French Atlantic Affair* and *Farewell Performance*) as well as a dozen or so short stories. Like Roger Thornhill, the characters in his fiction are urban dwellers, usually New Yorkers. They have an easy familiarity with the city, moving confidently through the streets and giving cab drivers precise instructions on how to navigate routes. Compare Roger Thornhill telling the driver to "make it the Fifty-Ninth Street entrance" of the Plaza with Sidney Falco in *Sweet Smell of Success* asking his cab driver, "Wait a minute…do you mind going by way of Fifty-fourth Street?" (p. 22). Just as Thornhill's conversation is sprinkled with specific references to New York locations so too is the short fiction. Al Preston in *The Comedian*, for example, looks for an acquaintance by calling "Sardi's, Shor's, Moore's, the Stage Delicatessen and Hanson's Drugstore" (p. 150).

Constantly on the move and on the make, Lehman's main characters are thirty to forty something males wielding power or looking to achieve it. In *Sweet Smell of Success* and the short story "Hunsecker Fights the World," J.J. Hunsecker is a ruthless gossip columnist; in *The Comedian* Sammy Hogarth is a domineering Sid Caesar-like television comic; in "Don't You Like It Out Here?" Finn Wildbeck is a manipulative studio boss. Orbiting around them are various wannabe press agents, publicists and gag writers.

Like Thornhill, these characters are often seen making multiple decisions on the run and barking instructions to female secretaries. Hurrying from his office building to the Plaza, Thornhill dictates two notes, a phone message and a self memo to his secretary Maggie who then reminds him of the following day's schedule: "Bigelow at ten-thirty is your first for tomorrow. You're due at the Skin Glow rehearsal at noon, then lunch with Falcon and his wife." The frantic exchange of information is much like that between press agent Sidney Falco and his secretary Gloria in "It's the Little Things that Count":

> "All rightie," Gloria said. "A note from Thelma Lance: 'Sidney: Don't be such a damned puritan. Call me.'"
> "No answer."
> I'd have to go into training first.
> "Morgan Wright sent back all the Friday copy…the Wilson Mizner anecdotes, the Truman gag and the — "
> "What about the plug for Wildbeck?"
> Fear suddenly twinged in my stomach.
> "That came back too. There's a note attached: 'Sorry, kiddie, but you know I don't go for mildew.'"
> I swore into the pillow.
> "Switch the Mizner stuff to the present tense, make it the other night at Twenty-One and credit Gene Fowler. And on the other, take out Truman and have George S. Kaufman say it about Russell Crouse. Send them to Elwell…" (p. 226)

There is humor in the conversations of Lehman's alphas and it is usually the barbed kind played out at someone else's expense. "The three of you together," Thornhill says to Vandamm, Leonard and Eve. "Now that's a picture only Charles Addams could draw." In one of his many insults, staff writer Sonny Carmichael greets Sammy Hogarth's younger brother Lester with "I was just wondering — does Sammy have you down as a dependent, or does he list you under contributions to charity?" (p. 132).

And when they are not rushing around grabbing power or destroying a rival, Lehman characters are drinking — in bars, hotel rooms, train cars, summer cottages and offices. Roger Thornhill tells the Professor he has several bartenders "dependent" on him and in "The Happy Hangover" faded actor Horace Paxton decides not to drop in at Paddy's bar because "Paddy could be awfully aggravating about a tiny pile of tabs" (p. 178).

Screenwriter Ernest Lehman wrote the scripts of North by Northwest *and* Family Plot.

Truth is neither absolute nor binding in this environment. "Ah, Maggie," Thornhill tells his secretary, "in the world of advertising there is no such thing as a lie. There is only The Expedient Exaggeration, you ought to know that." In "It's the Little Things that Count," Sidney Falco similarly tells his assistant, "There's no such thing as no news. You can always invent it" (p. 235). As a notoriously corrupt press agent, Falco takes credit for successes he did not influence, ascribes quotes to non-existent sources, plants inaccurate publicity items and spreads career-destroying rumors to curry favor with the victim's enemies. Appearances are almost always deceiving. Television personality Sammy Hogarth seems like a genial and generous funnyman but is actually an egotistical monster who physically abuses women and humiliates his family. Vic, the main character in "Clear Connection," pretends to be looking out for the wife of his wartime buddy Steve even though he is actually having an affair with her. Roy Samson, in "You Can't Have Everything," romances Marsha Cornell in order to get a piece of her millionaire father's fortune. J.J. Hunsecker and Sidney Falco continually proclaim their loyalty to people whom they are secretly plotting to betray.

Like the Vandamm-Leonard association in *North by Northwest*, a central dynamic in Lehman's fiction is the relationship between an oppressive kingpin and his sycophantic underling. These dysfunctional alliances, reminiscent of those between a prison boss and his punk or a Renaissance Pope and his cardinals, occur over and over. Falco performs Hunsecker's vindictive dirty work in order to get positive notices for his clients in Hunsecker's popular gossip column. Al Preston covers up Hogarth's (and his own) scandals to maintain his job as Hogarth's head comedy writer. As publicist at Finn Wildbeck's studio, Harry Bliss procures young women for Wildbeck in exchange for a promise to one day be made a screenwriter. Control is leveraged through verbal, economic and even physical intimidation. "I think you're jealous. No, I mean it. I am very touched. Very," taunts Vandamm just before punching Leonard in the face for proving Eve's disloyalty. *The Comedian* begins similarly as Hogarth spars aggressively with a physically overmatched Preston during a gym workout. Pounding away while he shouts out a litany of grievances, Hogarth ends by asking Preston, "I just hope you appreciate everything…Do you, Al,…I said *do* you?" (p. 126). It is the same question with the same implied threat of job loss that Wildbeck directs at Harry Bliss as prelude to his demand that a new starlet be lined up for his pleasure. "Don't you like it out here?" he asks Bliss. "… do you enjoy the climate, and the convertible you drive, and the charge account at Dick Carroll's, and the steaks at Chasen's, and the wild rice at LaRue's?" (p. 71). To maintain their always tenuous place in the hierarchy, Leonard goes on lighting Vandamm's cigarettes, Falco slouches out of a no-hit baseball game in the ninth inning because Hunsecker wants to make a point and Al Preston continues to tag along when Hogarth needs company on his midnight rambles around Manhattan.

Counter to these toxic codependencies are the romances in Lehman's work. As lovers, his flawed male characters struggle to find and express their best qualities. Harry Bliss falls for Rosemary Cobb, the young actress he is supposed to be making available for Wildbeck; Al Preston secretly marries Hogarth's secretary Connie; even Sidney Falco has an admirer in Hunsecker's secretary Mary. Note Lehman's failure to give surnames to the secretaries. Never fully developed, the female characters serve as fixed signifiers, representing unconditional acceptance, sincere encouragement and alternative life choices for the men. They are not made equal partners but the women are given resourcefulness and wit. A Lehman-written affair often begins with affectionate verbal banter between a cynical man and a clever woman. "Think how lucky I am to have been seated here," Thornhill tells Eve as he is shown to her table. "Oh, luck had nothing to do with it," she replies. "I tipped the steward five dollars to seat you here if you should come in." In a similar scene early in "You Can't Have Everything," Roy Samson sits down next to Ursula Wynant at a party and casually asks, "You mind?" "It's too early to tell," she answers (p. 90). As the relationships deepen, the men are forced to decide between committed love and compromised ambition.

Like the plot of *North by Northwest*, Lehman's fiction moves rapidly. Constructed primarily of dialogue, the stories contain few interior reflections and minimal description. Exposition and back-story are presented early and directly, almost mechanically. Thornhill sets the mistaken identity device in motion within minutes by telling his associates at the Plaza, "Oh, I just did something pretty stupid. I told my secretary to call Mother, and I realized she won't be able to reach her where she is…one of those new apartments — all wet paint and no phone yet…perhaps if I sent a telegram." Roy Samson explains his motivation on the second page: "The old guy had it all right — plenty of it — and a lot of it would be mine someday, just as soon as I popped the proper question. The only trouble was, it would be a package deal, and Marsha came in the package" (p. 90). Harry Bliss communicates his ambition in the opening paragraphs: "One of these days I was going to surprise her…because then I'd be rich and a successful writer instead of a mediocre studio press agent going nowhere" (p. 70).

Resolution of the power quest and the love affair, often interwoven and working against each other, comes quickly. Some of the men are redeemed. Roger Thornhill risks his life to rescue Eve. Harry Bliss rips a cigar out of Finn Wildbeck's mouth and leaves with the girl. Al Preston abandons Sammy Hogarth and walks "outside, into the fresh air" (p. 176) with his wife. On the other hand, Sidney Falco, conniving and dishonest to the end, turns his back on love and is destroyed by his greed. For all their world weariness and sophistication, Lehman's stories, like *North by Northwest* itself, are actually modern morality tales. Personal integrity, they caution, must always check ambition and, echoing Forster, individuals should "just connect" to find some measure of happiness in a corrupted world.

23: TWO TRAINS RUNNING

Whether intentional or coincidental, *North by Northwest* shares some striking similarities with *The Narrow Margin*, that powerful little RKO B-picture released in 1952. It is not possible to determine for sure if Hitchcock and/or Lehman saw the RKO film but to me it seems a real probability — especially since *The Narrow Margin* was very well received at the time by both critics and audiences.

Written by Earl Felton from a story by Martin Goldsmith and Jack Leonard and directed by Richard Fleischer, *The Narrow Margin* is the quintessential train thriller. The basic plot involves an attempt by a pair of LA cops to protect a gangster's widow turned grand jury witness from various mob hit men as she travels by train from Chicago to Los Angeles. As in *North by Northwest*, characters are not really who they appear to be. Frankie Neall's trampy, tough-talking widow (Marie Windsor at her best) is really undercover policewoman Sarah Meggs; Ann Sinclair (Jacqueline White), the proper single mom traveling with her precocious son Tommy and his nanny, is really the gangster's widow; and a disgruntled obese passenger turns out to be railroad security agent Sam Jennings (Paul Maxey). The hero (who also conceals his own identity) trying to sort out all the masquerades and do his job is terse, hard-boiled Detective Sergeant Walter Brown (*film noir* veteran Charles McGraw).

Nearly an hour of *The Narrow Margin*'s seventy-one minute running time occurs on board the train or in the railway stations; by comparison, about twenty-five minutes of *North by Northwest* takes place on the train or in the terminals. Both films share a similar attention to detail and a realistic sense of space in their treatment of the train scenes. As McGraw and Windsor arrive at the Chicago station, the off-screen public address system clearly announces their train as the "Golden West Limited departing track 8 in five minutes." We further know that they have been booked into Car Ten, Rooms A and B. Similarly, the first aural cue at Grand

Central Station is an off-screen announcement regarding the train that Thornhill will sneak aboard — "Train number twenty-five, the Twentieth-Century Limited, due to leave at six p.m., for Chicago, will depart on track number…." During the dining car scene, Eve tells Thornhill that she is in "Drawing room E. Car thirty-nine oh one." In both films, redcaps (train station porters) figure significantly in the action; McGraw arranges for a redcap to place his suitcases back on board the next westbound train as he arrives from Los Angeles with his partner to pick up Mrs. Neall, and Thornhill bribes a redcap for his uniform as a way to evade the police when he and Eve arrive in Chicago. *The Narrow Margin* correctly casts the redcap as African American since this was primarily a black labor union whereas Hitchcock fudges historical accuracy in order to make the impersonation gimmick work. Other operational details are also foregrounded to build verisimilitude and move the stories forward. In *The Narrow Margin*, telegrams are dispatched, mail is swung onboard as the train speeds through rural sidings and room assignments are checked by the conductor. In *North by Northwest*, Eve steals the porter's key to conceal Thornhill in an upper berth and Thornhill hides in the toilet as the conductor and his assistant move through the cars checking tickets.

Thornhill and Eve's mutual attraction to each other begins to play out when they are seated across from each other in the dining car. Walter Brown's interest in Ann Sinclair, whose blond elegance anticipates Eve's, happens in the same way. Even the seating arrangements for both couples are identical; the men sit on the left side of the frame and the women on the right. None of the four is initially honest about his or her true identity and intentions, but the romantic infatuation is conveyed through coded glances and gestures (Eve's suggestive caress of Thornhill's hand when he lights her cigarette is performed by Marie Windsor instead of love interest Jacqueline White in *The Narrow Margin*).

More significant is the way both films convey the claustrophobic space of the two trains. Unlike, say, the absurdly large club car that Edmond O'Brien visits in *The Killers*, the compartments and corridors of *The Narrow Margin* and *North by Northwest* are realistically tight. Sarah Meggs (as a decoy for Mrs. Neall) is hiding from the mob and Thornhill is hiding from the authorities. Their options, reflected in the constricted onboard space they inhabit, are severely limited. Both characters use restrooms as hiding places and hustle through the corridors to stay out of sight. Referencing the spatial as well as the temporal implications of its title, *The Narrow Margin* repeatedly has overweight rail agent Sam Jennings stand aside so that other passengers can squeeze past him in the passage ways. The presence in both films of a sizeable number of extras waiting for dining accommodations or grouped around exits further emphasizes the cramped *mise-en-scenes*. Reduced to the most constricted space possible, Thornhill hunkers down in the locked upper berth of Eve Kendall's sleeping compartment just as Sarah Meggs tries to confuse the hitmen following her by making them think she is stowed away inside the upper

Marie Windsor is menaced within the claustrophobic sleeping compartment of The Narrow Margin.

berths of Rooms A and B. Camera compositions inside the compartments of both films are set up to emphasize the berths looming in the upper halves of the frames. Fleischer further suggests confinement with lots of tight hand-held camera shots while Hitchcock relies on lighting and camera position to convey spatial restriction.

In contrast, frequent cutaways to the trains passing through dark landscapes allude to the wider yet still dangerous worlds and the broader options from which Thornhill, Meggs, Mrs. Neal and Brown are excluded. Hitchcock's cutaways are especially adroit — mounted on the outside of one of the cars, the camera shows the train rounding a bend and then pans to the right across a dark area which covers the transition to an ongoing pan into the train's interior. As the trains travel through space, the cutaways and the rear projections behind the car windows also orient us geographically. On route from Chicago to Los Angeles, the Golden West Limited is always shown moving from screen right to screen left. In adherence to the conventions of classic Hollywood cinema, the westward bound New York to Chicago Twentieth-Century Limited logically would be advancing in the same way, but Hitchcock must be concentrating on its run northward through the Hudson Valley since the screen direction is lower left frame to upper center.

Classic train comedies like *The Palm Beach Story*, *Twentieth Century* and *Some Like It Hot* take their time getting from point A to point B. There are no threatening deadlines nor doubts about whether the characters will arrive alive at their destinations. *North by Northwest*, however, is all about timelines and tension. In order to find George Kaplan and clear his name, Thornhill needs to make it to Chicago without getting caught by the authorities just as Walter Brown must get Mrs. Neall to the grand jury in Los Angeles before either of them is killed by mob assassins. Both men are vulnerable on board the Limited trains that appropriately limit their survival options as well.

Gritty where *North by Northwest* is glamorous, *The Narrow Margin* is a worthy precursor to Hitchcock's film and a likely influence on its pace and structure.

24: ARS GRATIA ARTIS

The United Nations Headquarters compound, featuring the 39-story Oscar Niemeyer-Le Corbusier designed Secretariat Building, was completed in 1952. The first major International Style skyscraper constructed in New York City, the Secretariat Building awed art critics with the way its green glass curtain wall, marble facade and bands of metal detailing combined into an organically sleek whole. It became an immediate architectural landmark and as recognizable a New York establishing shot icon as the Statue of Liberty or Empire State Building. Alfred Hitchcock, just seven years after its construction, was one of the first Hollywood directors to use the United Nations as a movie location. Showcasing its iconic distinction in a film which is full of references to art and which climaxes at equally famous Mount Rushmore (completed by sculptor Gutzon Borglum in 1941), Hitchcock turns the building into the most public and most unexpected of murder scenes.

Obtaining the site was difficult. Denied permission to film at the U.N., Hitchcock clandestinely photographed Cary Grant getting out of a cab and approaching the entrance and then cut to a meticulously reproduced lobby set in the studio. The scenic design features the real location's gleaming surfaces and expansive open spaces. After conversing with the receptionist, Thornhill proceeds to the public lounge where he has been told that Lester Townsend can be paged. The lounge set is vast and high-ceilinged with large windows looking out on a view of the East River and the Queensboro Bridge. There are leather chairs and sofas, low coffee tables, a cocktail bar, and, near the entranceway where Valerian lurks, a piece of modern sculpture. In this fashionably sleek setting, against a crowd of multiethnic faces, Thornhill pulls the knife from Townsend's back and gets blamed for his murder.

Another major architectural reference in *North by Northwest* is Frank Lloyd Wright. Vandamm's stunning cantilevered house, which we first see in a matted extreme long shot clinging to the hills around Mount Rushmore, is based on Wright designs like Fallingwater, Taliesin and the Sturges House in Brentwood Heights, not far from Hitchcock's home in Bel Air and a place with which art collector Hitchcock was surely familiar. Not only do the sharp angles, stone facades, split levels and sheer surfaces mesh with the visual design of the Mount Rushmore tourist center scenes but so also do they serve important plot functions. Thornhill scales the house's diagonal support beams to find Eve and utilizes the wraparound balcony overlooking the living room (a key feature of the Taliesin floor plan) to drop her the monogrammed matchbook warning that she has been made. There is an openness to the Vandamm house that is evident in most of the film's settings — the U.N. lobby and lounge, Grand Central Station, the Mount Rushmore observation deck and cafeteria and, of course, outdoor locations like Prairie Stop and the Mount Rushmore monument "exteriors." Open space is an essential element of both the film's aesthetic and its theme. Violence and danger, Hitchcock insists, do not just lurk in gloomy old houses and dark alleys but can swoop down suddenly from the empty expanses of a Midwestern sky or lash out from the periphery of a vast public forum dedicated to international peace. Thornhill in public may be even more vulnerable than Thornhill in private.

The geometric grid patterns of the U.N. Building and of Vandamm's cliffside house are anticipated in the introductory title sequence by Saul Bass. The intended effect is that the art is being created as we watch. An empty flat surface, pale green in color, opens the film. Then, as if being etched by an invisible pen, parallel lines stream across the frame from the right and intersect with another set of lines entering from above and below. Upon completion of the grid, words appear along the diagonals to convey the credit information. Later, the green surface transforms into the facade of a skyscraper and the diagonals become windows. Representative of the New York school of graphic design, Bass developed title sequences and/or advertising posters for major films by Hitchcock, Preminger, Kubrick, Scorsese and Wilder among others. His most famous work includes the credit/poster package for *The Man with the Golden Arm, Bonjour Tristesse, Vertigo, Exodus, Anatomy of a Murder* and *Advise and Consent*; titles for *The Big Knife, Psycho, Spartacus, West Side Story, Walk on the Wild Side* and *Goodfellas*; and posters for *Love in the Afternoon, One, Two, Three, The Firemen's Ball* and *The Shining*. In addition, Bass storyboarded *Psycho*'s shower sequence and was responsible for its overall rapid montage concept. As a whole, Bass's visual design for film is minimalistic and features jagged images, fragmented figures, stark cut-outs and off-kilter typography. Saul Bass and Associates (later renamed Saul Bass/ Herb Yearer and Associates) also designed the universally recognizable logos for AT&T, Continental Airlines, Minolta, United Airlines, Warner Communications, Avery International, Dixie, Celanese and many other corporations.

The United Nations lobby set epitomizes mid twentieth century interior design.

In *A History of Graphic Design,* Philip Meggs observes that Bass "frequently reduced his graphic designs to a single dominant image, often centered in the space" (p. 341). Saluting Bass's ability to capture thematic ideas in basic pictures, Meggs writes, "There is a robust energy about his forms and an almost casual quality about their execution. While images are simplified to a minimal statement, they lack the exactitude of measurement or construction that could make them rigid" (p. 342). The single striking image set within an austere compositional field is also characteristic of *North by Northwest's* specific painterly references. The painted glass process shot in which a tiny Thornhill runs past a fountain on a diagonal sidewalk at the very bottom of the Secretariat Building suggests surrealistic de Chirico landscapes like *Piazza d'Italia* or *The Enigma of a Day* in the way it extends perspective and foreshortens objects. Similarly, the chase across the giant Mount Rushmore faces evokes Dali (*Apparition of Face and Fruit, Dish on a Beach, The Endless Enigma*), Tanguy (*A Large Painting which is a Landscape*), Magritte (*The Double Secret*) and even Vincent Korda's art direction from 1940's *The Thief of Bagdad* (compare Sabu dangling from the face of the huge All-Seeing Eye statue with Cary Grant and Eva Marie Saint sliding down the smooth rocks adjacent to George Washington's chin).

Throughout *North by Northwest* there are an awareness and appreciation of fine art, fashion and design. Hotels, lounges and living rooms reflect the ideal of "flowing openness" which characterizes late 50s interior decoration, and the furniture is typically low slung, austere and sleek. Eve Kendall's costumes, originally designed by M-G-M's Harry Kress, were rejected by Hitchcock and supposedly then chosen by Eva Marie Saint and Hitchcock himself at Bergdorf Goodman. Eve first appears in a tailored black suit with a pencil skirt, catching Thornhill's attention as she walks the train corridor like a designer runway. She wears a black evening dress later for dinner in the dining car, a black and red rose print dress for the auction, a green suit at the Mount Rushmore cafeteria and a bright orange dress for the airplane flight out of Vandamm's Black Hills hideaway. The clothing is fashionably current — gowns low cut at the back; bare shoulders; man-tailored open box suits; evening gowns with neatly molded bodices and full skirts; silk damask materials in rich prints; and the use of greens and reds as popular designer colors. The immaculate hair is nape length, slightly bobbed and waved back away from the forehead. When Eve, Thornhill and Vandamm gather at the Shaw and Oppenheim Galleries, Hitchcock is very specific about the *objets d'art* being auctioned. Along with the pre-Columbian Tarascan Warrior Statuette that Vandamm purchases, there are Louis Seize fauteuils, an Aubusson settee, collector's porcelain, an early seventeenth-century painting and a carved and gilded Louis Quinze *lit de repos*. The original script also lists an eighteenth-century hand-carved barometer, a Louis Quinze Curio Cabinet of gold and bronze dore with Vernis Martin figured decorations, a Marcolini Meissen compote and twelve Royal Vienna plates. Together they form a miscellany of the kinds of artifacts rich Americans were displaying in their homes circa 1959.

The auction sequence makes it clear that art exists simultaneously on two levels — as commodity and as creative expression. It is with this argument that Hitchcock offers up the film itself. Working at the height of his artistic powers, he is midway in a string of masterworks that ultimately also will include *Rear Window, Vertigo, Psycho* and *The Birds*. As dazzling as the art it references, *North by Northwest* pops and shimmers with rich Technicolor visuals. Financed at his largest budget yet, it is a compendium of everything Hitchcock has learned about filmmaking — how camera movement conveys meaning, how images form a conceptual pattern, how framing reveals character. It is a bid for marketplace success and also for the critical respect as an artist that Hitchcock deserves as much or more than any other Hollywood studio director.

25: FINALE

Except for a handful of misfires like *Jamaica Inn* and *Under Capricorn*, Hitchcock's films are not dated. *North by Northwest* wears especially well. In fact, it seems to get better upon repeat viewings, communicating a continuously contemporary look and tone. The clothes are classically stylish, the jokes still work, the performances are unaffectedly smooth and the music is urgent without being over the top. Cary Grant never looked more handsome, Eva Marie Saint more elegant nor James Mason more dangerously debonair. The New York City that Hitchcock celebrates may have changed but is still recognizable to us in its energy and its architectural flair.

In many ways the paradigmatic summer action blockbuster, *North by Northwest* hurtles forward at a pace so brisk it practically gets ahead of itself. Shot/reverse shot conversations are cut crisply on ending and beginning syllables, and word bridges almost subliminally elide two successive shots. As Roger Thornhill rushes to beat a series of interlocking deadlines, the narrative races from one suspenseful turning point to another. Always, a verbal clue or a physical trigger projects rapidly forward from segment A to segment B and then from B to C and so on. With a "running" time of 136 minutes, *North by Northwest* is Hitchcock's longest film but feels like one of his shortest.

On multiple occasions, Ernest Lehman mentioned that in writing *North by Northwest* he was striving to create the quintessential Hitchcock romantic thriller. Certainly there is that cachet to the film. Combining the plots of *Notorious* and *The 39 Steps*, Lehman deepened the character analysis while blurring the moral distinction between opposing sides in the intelligence war. Skilled at creating brittle dialogue that thrusts and parries for advantage, he added urban sophistication and a cynical sense of the speciousness of mass media and advertising. And then he pumped up the trademark Hitchcock features — more elaborate set pieces, more locations, bigger crowds, better special effects, a nonstop chase and more sex. Hitchcock's cameo appearance is funnier and more self-effacing than usual, and there are plentiful examples of Hitchcock's fondness for subtle dark humor, like staging a murder in a place devoted to world peace or positioning the most treacherous of the villains to descend Mount Rushmore next to the profile of "honest" Abe Lincoln. *North by Northwest* also boasts the distinction of having the flimsiest of all MacGuffins[1] in the microfilm-laced statue and the iciest of all Hitchcock blondes in the duplicitous Eve Kendall.

Everyone involved with *North by Northwest* is working at the top of his game. M-G-M's production budget and technical resources are well used. Sets for the United Nations lobby, Townsend library, hotel rooms, train interiors, auction gallery, Vandamm retreat and Mount Rushmore itself are convincingly realistic, a significantly ironic attribute for a film which otherwise undermines the reliability of appearance. The process photography, which can sometimes be sloppy in Hitchcock, is immaculate. Compare, for example, the awkward rear projections of Melanie Daniels crossing Bodega Bay in her rented motorboat with the seamless ones of Roger Thornhill and the Professor walking across the Chicago airport tarmac. Even the ambient details in *North by Northwest* are exactly right. The female public address announcer at the La Salle Street Station speaks with an authentic Chicago accent, and the busboy who witnesses the Mount Rushmore shooting for the radio report has the appropriately Scandinavian South Dakota name of Chris Swenson.

Casual film-goers who are not intimately familiar with Hitchcock's career know three Hitchcock films. They know *Psycho*, *The Birds* and *North by Northwest*. Maybe not the title exactly but they know they've seen it. "That's the one with Cary Grant in a suit being chased by an airplane, right?" they'll ask, or "It ends with Cary Grant and a pretty blonde hanging from the President's head," they will remember. And in those scraps of memory are keys to the film's wide popularity: Cary Grant; jaw-dropping, fast paced physical action; humor; glamour and scenic locales.

1. For those who need an explanation, the MacGuffin is Hitchcock's term for the plot device, often outlandish and sometimes meaningless, that motivates the characters' actions. As Hitchcock tells it, two men are on a train to Scotland. One of the travelers asks the other what is inside the parcel he is carrying in the luggage rack. "Oh, that's a MacGuffin," answers the owner of the package. "What's a MacGuffin?" asks the inquisitor. "It's an apparatus for hunting lions in the Scottish highlands," answers the owner. "But there are no lions in the Scottish highlands," says the inquisitive traveler. "Oh, well then, that's no MacGuffin," says the owner.

Gus Van Sant, in 1998, famously and disastrously remade *Psycho*. Intended as a scene-for-scene homage, it was instead a botched pastiche. Anthony Perkins himself starred in two weak sequels, even directing the less accomplished of the pair. None of it worked, and the young mostly male audiences for which it was intended preferred to get their gore from the Jason, Michael and Freddy slasher franchises which Hitchcock's Ur-film had made possible in the first place. Ransacked rather than remade, *North by Northwest* also looms large in the collective imagination of filmmakers. The sardonically capable hero, suave villain, compromised eleventh hour heroine, outrageous physical stunts and travelogue photography of every James Bond film ever made stem from *North by Northwest*. So too the mistaken identity device in films as disparate as *The Passenger* and *The Man with One Red Shoe*. Roger Thornhill is also there in men on the run like Jason Bourne and Joe Turner (Robert Redford) in *Three Days of the Condor*. Gene Wilder and Gilda Radner play the Cary Grant and Eva Marie Saint parts in a forgotten 1982 spy chasing escapade called *Hanky Panky*, and Ernest Lehman even cribbed from himself for character traits and plot details in *The Prize*.

Coming in 1959 on that same creative threshold that will mark many of the most unique masterpieces in French and Italian cinema, *North by Northwest* has a distinct modernist sensibility to it. Dissolute ad man Roger Thornhill pinned against a barren landscape evokes a tableau from "The Hollow Men." The empty alienated space also suggests Antonioni, as does Hitchcock's carefully coded use of color, especially the cool blues punctuated by a warning flash of red. Recurrent pictorial reflections like those in the opening credits, train windows, Vandamm television screen and intelligence agency plaque play with the difference between reality and appearance, substance and illusion. By incriminating Thornhill with a misleading newspaper picture which shows him pulling a knife from Townsend's lifeless body, Hitchcock calls into question, just as Godard will in a series of increasingly non-narrative films, the representational ontology of the photographic image itself. The world of *North by Northwest* is reminiscent of Pirandello, Kafka and Beckett. Elusive if not unobtainable, truth is a constantly constructed fiction. Characters tear away one clouded screen only to have another equally convincing one appear. There are too many intervening forces to make direct perception anything other than directed observation.

North by Northwest also expresses a delight in making movies as overwhelming as that of a Fellini or a Truffaut. Remember Lehman wanting to write the perfect Hitchcock film or remember Hitchcock telling Lehman, "I always wanted to do something involving a chase across Mount Rushmore" (Brady, p. 187). There is a sense of technical limits pushed and budget constraints ignored. The exhilaration of *North by Northwest* is, I believe, Hitchcock's own personal one as well. His wife Alma had beaten her cancer diagnosis, MCA was negotiating lucrative contracts for him, the television series was a financial success and the cast and crew were deferentially professional. Maybe most importantly of all for Hitchcock, his leading lady cooperated fully with his directives in a working relationship that was productive and without trauma.

We return to Hitchcock for many reasons. In *Vertigo* we return to behold the dark night of a soul fated to relive the loss of that which it desires most intensely. *Psycho* wrenches us each time with its utter hopelessness, its harsh denial of narrative expectations and its elemental brutality. *The Birds* is an apocalyptic cautionary tale, playing out the collapse of order on cosmic and personal levels. *North by Northwest* is something different. We return, as in a frequent nightmare, to loss of self, exclusion from society and pursuit. We return for primal fears, betrayal and redemption. Above all, we return to experience again why we love movies in general and Hitchcock in particular.

And so, fittingly, timpani crescendo.

Train enters tunnel.

The end.

The film's sexually suggestive final shot is Hitchcock's humorous response to the censors.

Appendix A: ROGER THORNHILL'S APPOINTMENTS

DAY 1

Afternoon: *drinks with Herman Weltner and clients at the Plaza*

mistaken for George Kaplan and kidnapped

Evening: *interrogated by Vandamm at Townsend mansion*

force fed bourbon and arrested by Glen Cove police for drunk driving

night in jail

DAY 2

Morning: *court hearing in Glen Cove on DUI charge; case held over until 7:30 p.m. next day*

return to Townsend mansion with lawyer and court officials; no evidence of Vandamm found

Afternoon: *meet mother to search George Kaplan room at Plaza Hotel*

taxi to United Nations Building to interview Lester Townsend; implicated in Townsend's murder

Evening: *un-ticketed 6 p.m. boarding of Twentieth-Century Limited to Chicago*

dinner with Eve Kendall in dining car

night in Eve Kendall's sleeping compartment

DAY 3

Morning: *9 a.m. arrival at La Salle Street Station, Chicago; disguised exit with Eve Kendall*

Afternoon: *arrival by bus in Prairie Stop at approximately 3:30 p.m.; survival of crop-dusting attack and return to Chicago by stolen truck*

Evening: *shower and shave in Eve Kendall's room at Ambassador East Hotel*

meeting with Vandamm, Leonard and Eve at Shaw and Oppenheim Galleries, Chicago

disruption and arrest by Chicago police

flight to Rapid City, South Dakota, with Professor on Northwest Orient Airlines

night in transit

DAY 4

Afternoon: *meeting with Vandamm, Leonard and Eve at Mount Rushmore cafeteria; faked shooting by Eve*

meeting with Eve and Professor in forest at Black Hills; subdued by park ranger and taken to Rapid City Hospital

Evening: *escape from hospital*

arrival at Vandamm's home near Mount Rushmore

rescue of Eve and chase across monument; saved from fall by Professor and park police

return to New York from Chicago on Twentieth-Century Limited (perhaps Day 5)

Appendix B: THE SHOOT

North by Northwest was filmed from August 27, 1958, to December 24, 1958. It premiered in Chicago, was released nationally in July, 1959, and opened on August 6, 1959, at Radio City Music Hall, where it had a then record-breaking engagement.

The only film Hitchcock ever made for M-G-M, *North by Northwest* was initially budgeted at around $3.1 million but ultimately climbed to about $4.3 million. In the middle of one of its recurrent post war administrative reorganizations and headed at the time by Sol Siegel, the studio interfered surprisingly little with the film and gave producer-director Hitchcock most everything he wanted, including Cary Grant and Eva Marie Saint as stars instead of the studio-proposed casting of Gregory Peck and Cyd Charisse. Hitchcock was paid $250,000 plus 10% of the gross over $8 million. Cary Grant received $450,000 up front, a share of the profits, and $5,000 per each day beyond the contracted shooting schedule. Since that schedule had nearly elapsed before shooting began and because the film garnered a sizeable profit ($6.5 million box office in North America alone), Cary Grant took home a great deal of money for his performance in *North by Northwest*. For writing the original script, Ernest Lehman was paid $25,000.

Working in VistaVision and Technicolor, Hitchcock shot on location from August to September and in the studio from September until late December. Locations included New York City, Long Island, Chicago, Mount Rushmore and central California. In New York City, Hitchcock filmed in the lobby of the Plaza Hotel and at Grand Central Station. Denied permission to shoot inside the United Nations Building, he picked up footage of Cary Grant arriving by cab at the U.N. entrance and then reconstructed the visitors' lobby in the studio. The Oak Room Bar and Kaplan hotel room interiors were also shot in the studio. For the Townsend mansion exteriors, Hitchcock used the Phipps Estate in Old

Westbury, New York, and then built the Townsend library set on a sound stage. In Chicago, filming took place at the La Salle Street Station and the Ambassador East Hotel lobby. Since the National Park Service severely restricted Hitchcock's use of the Mount Rushmore locale, he filmed on the observation deck and in the parking lot and then famously built massive replicas of the Presidential heads in the studio for the climactic chase scene. Other studio sets included the train interiors, Eve's hotel room, the art auction, the Black Hills forest rendezvous and Vandamm's mountain retreat.

The classic Prairie Stop, Indiana, crop-dusting scene was actually filmed north of Bakersfield, California, near the tiny towns of Wasco and Delano. The crossroads is just east of the intersection of Corcoran Road and Highway 155. The dried-out cornfield was "planted" by the prop department; studio inserts of Thornhill hiding among the corn stalks were intercut with the location shots. Temperatures during the late summer filming exceeded 100° F in the shade.

A rough cut of *North by Northwest* was screened for the M-G-M Board of Directors in late April, 1959. The studio, Siegel in particular, thought the film was too long at 136 minutes and wanted to cut the scene where Thornhill and Eve reunite in the Black Hills. Hitchcock's MCA-negotiated contract gave him control of the final edit, he refused and the scene remained. Hitchcock received considerably more interference from Geoffrey Shurlock, head of the Production Code Administration, who objected to Leonard's sexuality, Thornhill's multiple marriages and the steamy Twentieth-Century Limited scenes. Giving in only slightly, Hitchcock had Eva Marie Saint re-dub her line "I never make love on an empty stomach" to "I never discuss love on an empty stomach" and added "Come along Mrs. Thornhill" to the sleeping compartment transition to indicate that Roger and Eve had been married. The final coital image of the train entering a tunnel was Hitchcock's revenge.

Alternate titles proposed for *North by Northwest* were *Breathless, In a Northwesterly Direction, The Man on Lincoln's Nose, It's Good to be Alive* and *The Bed That Wasn't Slept In*. Titles for the foreign market releases included *Der Unsichtbare Dritte (The Invisible Third Person), Das Erbe des Grauens (Heritage of Fear), La Mort aux Trousses (Death at the Heels)* and *Intrigo Internazionale (International Intrigue)*.

At the 32nd Annual Academy Awards, *North by Northwest* was nominated for but did not win best art direction, best screenplay and best editing. Hitchcock also received a Directors Guild nomination. Among the honors won by *North by Northwest* were the San Sebastian Film

Festival's Best Film award, the Edgar Allen Poe Award for best film and the Writers Guild award for best comedy.

In 1995, *North by Northwest* was added to the National Registry by the National Film Preservation Board.

Appendix C: CREDITS

CREW

Producer-Director	Alfred Hitchcock
Production Company	Metro-Goldwyn-Mayer
Screenplay	Ernest Lehman
Music	Bernard Herrmann
Director of Photography	Robert Boyle
Art Direction	William A. Horning
	Merrill Pye
Set Decoration	Henry Grace
	Frank McKelvey
Special Effects	A. Arnold Gillespie
	Lee LeBlanc
Titles	Saul Bass
Film Editor	George Tomasini
Color Consultant	Charles K. Hagedon
Recording Supervisor	Franklin Milton
Hair Styles	Sydney Guilaroff
Make-up	William Tuttle
Assistant Director	Robert Saunders
Associate Producer	Herbert Coleman

CAST

Roger Thornhill	Cary Grant
Eve Kendall	Eva Marie Saint
Phillip Vandamm	James Mason

Clara Thornhill	Jessie Royce Landis
The Professor	Leo G. Carroll
Leonard	Martin Landau
Licht	Robert Ellenstein
Valerian	Adam Williams
Vandamm's Sister	Josephine Hutchinson
Captain Junket (Glen Cove)	Edward Binns
Sergeant Emil Klinger	John Beradino
Out of Town Clients	Robert Shayne Carleton Young
Judge	Alexander J. Lockwood
Lester Townsend	Philip Ober
Thornhill's Lawyer	Edward Platt
Housekeeper (Anna)	Nora Marlowe
Maggie	Doreen Lang
Maid (Elsie)	Maudie Prickett
Valet	James McCallion
Auctioneer	Les Tremayne
Ticket Agent	Ned Glass
Man on Highway 41	Malcolm Atterbury
Herman Weltner	Frank Wilcox
Night Court Doctor	Philip Coolidge
Chicago Policemen	Patrick McVey Ken Lynch
Assistant Auctioneer	Olan Soule

WORKS CITED

Barton, Sabrina. "Hitchcock's Hands," *2000-01 Hitchcock Annual* (p. 2000), 47-72.

Brady, John. "An Interview with Ernest Lehman," in James Naremore (ed.), *North by Northwest, Alfred Hitchcock, Director*. New Brunswick, New Jersey: Rutgers University Press, 1993, pp. 186-90.

Brill, Lesley. *The Hitchcock Romance: Love and Irony in Hitchcock's Films*. Princeton, New Jersey: Princeton University Press, 1988.

Campbell, Joseph. *The Hero with a Thousand Faces*. New York: MJF Books, 1949.

Doty, Alexander. *Flaming Classics: Queering the Film Canon*. New York: Routledge, 2000.

Hamill, Pete. *A Drinking Life: A Memoir*. Boston: Little, Brown and Company, 1994.

Hayward, Susan. *Key Concepts in Cinema Studies*. London: Routledge, 1996.

Kael, Pauline. *I Lost It At The Movies*. Boston: Little, Brown and Company, 1965.

Keane, Marian. "The Designs of Authorship: An Essay on *North by Northwest*" in James Naremore (ed.), *North by Northwest, Alfred Hitchcock, Director*. New Brunswick, New Jersey: Rutgers University Press, 1993, pp. 210-20.

LaValley, Albert J. *Focus on Hitchcock*. Englewood Cliffs, New Jersey: Prentice-Hall, Inc., 1972.

Laverty, Chris. *"North by Northwest: Cary Grant's Kilgour Suit,"* http://www.clothesonfilm.com/cary-grant-grey-Kilgour-suit-in-north.../844 (May 13, 2009).

Lehman, Ernest. *North by Northwest: A Viking Film Book*. New York: The Viking Press, 1972.

Lehman, Ernest. *Sweet Smell of Success: The Short Fiction of Ernest Lehman*. Woodstock, New York: The Overlook Press, 2000.

McBride, Joseph. *Searching for John Ford: A Life*. London: Faber and Faber, 2003.

McEwen, Todd. "Cary Grant's Suit," *Selected Shorts, Adventures in London and the Wild West*, Public Radio International Podcast, November 23, 2009.

McGilligan, Patrick. *Alfred Hitchcock: A Life in Darkness and Light*. New York: Regan Books, 2003.

Meggs, Philip B. *A History of Graphic Design*, third edition. New York: John Wiley and Sons, Inc., 1998.

Mulvey, Laura. *Visual and Other Pleasures*. Bloomington, Indiana: Indiana University Press, 1989.

Naremore, James (ed.) *North by Northwest, Alfred Hitchcock, Director*. New Brunswick, New Jersey: Rutgers University Press, 1993, continuity script pp. 35-172.

Russo, Vito. *The Celluloid Closet*, Revised edition. New York: Harper and Row, Publishers, 1987.

Sullivan, Jack. *Hitchcock's Music*. New Haven, Connecticut: Yale University Press, 2006.

Thomson, David. *The New Biographical Dictionary of Film*. New York: Alfred A. Knopf, 2002.

Torregrossa, Richard. "Cary Grant and the Secrets of the Perfect Suit," *www.RichardTorregrossa.com/Cary-Grant-and-the-secrets-of-the-perfect-suit.htm*.

Truffaut, Francois. *Hitchcock*. New York: Simon and Schuster, 1967.

Wakefield, Dan. *New York in the Fifties*. Boston: Houghton Mifflin/Seymour Lawrence, 1992.

Williams, William Carlos. *Paterson*. New York: New Directions, 1963.

Wollen, Peter. *Readings and Writings: Semiotic Counter-Strategies*. London: Verso, 1982.

INDEX

Academy Awards 16, 108, 109, 182
Addams, Charles 138, 158
Addison, John 149
Advise and Consent 168
Affleck, Ben 113
Aldrich, Robert 101
All About Eve 99
Alternate titles for *NbN* 42, 148, 182
Ambassador East Hotel 31, 54, 71, 83, 84, 85, 151, 179, 182
American Film Institute 16
Anatomy of a Murder 108, 168
Antonioni, Michelangelo 175
Arthur, Jean 107
Artist, The 149
Astaire, Fred 128
Atterbury, Malcolm 121

Balsam, Martin 45, 122
Bankhead, Tallulah 54, 107
Barton, Sabrina 57, 59
Bass, Saul 41, 168, 169
Battleship Potemkin 115
Beckett, Samuel 175
Ben-Hur 16, 108
Bennett, Constance 107
Bergman, Ingrid 18, 105, 106, 107
Big Knife, The 168
Big Sleep, The 119
Birds, The 15, 16, 17, 43, 53, 69, 77, 140, 148, 149, 154, 171, 174, 176
Black Sunday 157
Blindfold 108

Bogart, Humphrey 111
Bond, James 102, 108, 175
Bonjour Tristesse 168
Borglum, Gutzon 145, 167
Boyle, Robert 145
Breakfast at Tiffany's 70, 111
Breathless 113
Brill, Lesley 63, 64
Bringing up Baby 105, 147
Brynner, Yul 95
Burgess, Guy 101
Burks, Robert 15, 70
Burton, Tim 155

Caesar, Sid 158
Calhern, Louis 49
Campbell, Joseph 64, 80
Caron, Leslie 107
Carroll, Leo G. 102, 105
Carroll, Lewis 14, 128
Carroll, Madeleine 47
Carson, Rachel 131
Cartwright, Veronica 77
Casablanca 53, 111, 115
Casino Royale 132
Cat Ballou 73
Chambers, Whittaker 101
Charade 25, 108
Charisse, Cyd 181
Chirico, Giorgio di 170
Coburn, James 102
Collateral 113
Comedian, The 157-61

Connery, Sean 102
Cook, Elisha Jr. 97
Cooper, Gary 108
Corbusier, Le 167
Craig, Daniel 102
Crain, Jeanne 107
Crime of Passion 121
Cromwell, James 113
Crosby, Bing 108
Cruise, Tom 113
Cummings, Robert 46, 55, 147

Dali, Salvador 170
Date with Judy, A 154
Day, Doris 102, 107, 154
Days of Wine and Roses 73
Depp, Johnny 108
Desert Fox, The 95
Desk Set 73
Dial M for Murder 48, 54, 55
Dietrich, Marlene 18, 107, 154
Donat, Robert 46, 55
Donen, Stanley 108
Doty, Alexander 99
Dr. No 108
Dunne, Irene 107

Edwards, Blake 155
8 ½ 113
Elfman, Danny 155
Eliot, T.S. 116, 175
Elliot, Laura 54
Evans, Walker 135
Executive Suite 157
Exodus 168

Family Plot 157
Fellini, Federico 175
Felton, Earl 163
Fields, W.C. 73
film noir 101, 119, 163
Firemen's Ball 168
Fitzgerald, F. Scott 116
Five Fingers 95
Fleischer, Richard 163

Fleming, Ian 101, 108
Fonda, Henry 14, 55, 154
Fontaine, Joan 106
Ford, John 73, 118
Foreign Correspondent 46, 47, 48, 55, 69, 101
Foreign titles for *NbN* 128, 182
Forster, E.M. 161
From Here to Eternity 111
From Here to Texas 121
From the Terrace 157
Frye, Northrup 63
Fuller, Sam 101

Gavin, John 17
Georgy Girl 95
Gilda 111
Godard, Jean Luc
Going My Way 108
Goldfinger 131
Goldsmith, Martin 163
Goodfellas 168
Grace, Henry 145
Grand Central Station 29, 54, 55, 69, 80, 108, 153, 154, 164, 168, 181
Granger, Farley 47, 105, 154
Grant, Cary 13, 27 48, 50, 54, 78, 88, 90, 95, 96, 101, 102, 128, 133, 134, 146, 147, 150 151, 154 167, 170, 174, 181
  acting talent 105, 106, 107, 108, 109, 118, 121
  career 24, 25, 89, 105, 107, 140
  leading ladies 107, 108
  movie star icon 87, 105, 108
  recognition 108, 109
  style 106, 111-13
Greene, Graham 15 101
Grosz, George 141
Gunga Din 25, 105, 140

Hamlet 17
Hamill, Pete 75
Hanky Panky 175
Hardwicke, Sir Cedric 55
Hardy, Oliver 120

INDEX

Harlow, Jean 107
Harvey 73
Harvey, Laurence 108
Hawks, Howard 27, 105, 109
Hayworth, Rita 111
Hedren, Tippi 15, 17, 53, 90, 105, 154
Hepburn, Audrey 107, 108, 111
Hepburn, Katharine 107, 147
Herrmann, Bernard 15, 149-55
Heston, Charlton 108
His Girl Friday 27, 105
Hitchcock, Alfred 13, 45, 46, 57, 94, 106, 107, 119, 120, 123, 126, 127, 132, 164, 166, 167, 173, 175, 181, 182
  collaboration with creative team 15, 145, 155, 157, 176
  recognition 16, 171, 182, 183
  relations with leading ladies 53, 85, 90, 91, 170, 176
  silent film influences 15, 40, 115, 146
  themes 16, 17, 18, 781, 77-78, 91, 96, 99, 100, 101, 105, 151, 168, 174
  time manipulation 27, 29, 30, 31, 32, 33, 124, 131
  urban settings 18, 56, 69-72
  use of objects 53-56, 59, 88, 90, 91
  use of sound 116, 118, 125, 130, 133, 134, 135, 144, 150, 154, 155
  visual style 15, 35-43, 84-91, 116, 117, 121, 122, 124, 130, 133, 136, 137-41, 143-48, 165
Hitchcock, Patricia 54
Hoffman Irving 157
Horning, William 145
Houseboat 25
How to Marry a Millionaire 70
Hudson, Rock 108

I Confess 69
Iles, Francis 106
Inspector Call, An 149
It's A Wonderful Life 73
It Should Happen to You 70
I Was a Male War Bride 106

Jamaica Inn 173

Kael, Pauline 95
Kafka, Franz 14, 175
Keane, Marian 21
Kelly, Gene 128
Kelly, Grace 15, 54, 55, 78, 105, 107
Kerr, Deborah 107
Kilgour, French and Stanbury 112
Killers, The 164
King and I, The 157
Kiss Me Deadly 101
Konstantin, Leopoldin 77
Korda, Vincent 170
Kress, Harry 170
Kruger, Otto 147
Kruschev, Nikita 101
Kubrick, Stanley 168

Lady Vanishes, The 15, 47, 101, 103
Lancaster, Burt 111
Landau, Martin 97, 147
Landis, Jessie Royce 78
Lane, Priscilla 46
Last Angry Man, The 108
Laura 98
LaValley, Albert 115
Laverty, Chris 111, 112
Le Carré, John 103
Lehman, Ernest 93, 97, 100, 105, 115, 134, 136, 148, 157-61, 173, 175, 181
Leigh Janet 15
Lemmon, Jack 108
Leonard, Jack 163
Leone, Sergio 155
Lifeboat 54, 83
Lolita 95
Lombard, Carole 107
Lorne, Marion 78
Lost Weekend 73
Love in the Afternoon 168
Loy, Myrna 13, 107
Lyons, Arthur 112

Maclean, Donald 101

Magritte, René 170
Maltese Falcon, The 97, 98
Mancini, Henry 155
Man from U.N.C.L.E., The 102
Man Who Knew Too Much, The (1934 version) 101
Man Who Knew Too Much, The (1956 version) 15, 47, 101, 102, 147, 154
Man with One Red Shoe, The 175
Man with the Golden Arm, The 168
Marnie 15, 149, 154
Martin, Dean 102
Mason, James 28, 90, 94, 95, 102, 106, 112, 173
Maxey, Paul 163
McCarey, Leo 109
McCrea, Joel 47, 70
McEwen, Todd 113
McGilligan, Patrick 90
McGraw, Charles 163
McKelvey Frank 145
Meggs, Philip 169
M-G-M 15, 90, 145, 170, 174, 181, 182
Miles, Vera 17
Mission Impossible 135, 148
Mitchum, Robert 108
Monkey Business 105
Moore, Roger 102
Morricone, Ennio 155
Mount Rushmore 13, 14, 15, 24, 25, 27, 33, 37, 39, 40, 41, 47, 49 51, 59, 63, 65, 66, 86, 88, 90 91, 93, 94, 97, 106, 111, 137, 143-48, 152, 154, 167, 168, 170, 174, 176, 179, 182
Mr. and Mrs. Smith 69
Mulvey, Laura 49, 86
Muni, Paul 108
Murder! 18, 99
My Favorite Year 70

Narrow Margin, The 163-66
Newman, Paul 108
Niemeyer, Oscar 167
Ninotchka 73
Niven, David 105

None but the Lonely Heart 106, 108
Notorious 15, 16, 18, 48-52, 53, 69, 77, 96, 99, 101, 105, 107, 173
Novak, Kim 15, 17, 45

O'Brien, Edmond 164
Ocean's 11 113
Odd Man Out 95
One, Two, Three 168
Only Angels Have Wings 105
On the Town 70
On the Waterfront 70
Out of the Past 119

Palm Beach Story, The 166
Pandora and the Flying Dutchman 95
Pangborn, Franklin 98
Paradine Case, The 55
Passenger, The 175
Paycheck 113
Peck, Gregory 181
Penny Serenade 108
Perkins, Anthony 17, 175
Philadelphia Story, The 105
Picasso, Pablo 45, 48
Pickup on South Street 101
Pirandello, Luigi 175
Plaza Hotel 14, 28, 35, 39, 55, 65, 66, 70, 78, 79, 94, 112, 154, 157, 158, 179 181
Potter, H.C. 13
Preminger, Otto 168
Previn, André 154
Pride and the Passion, The 25
Prize, The 157, 175
process shots 35, 71, 125, 127, 128, 134, 146, 174
Production Code Administration 87, 88, 182
Propp, Vladimir 63
Psycho 15, 16, 17, 45, 55, 56, 69, 78, 96, 99, 122, 149, 168, 171, 174, 175, 176
Purple Noon 113
Pye, Merrill 145

Radner, Gilda 175
Rains, Claude 18, 106
rear projection 15, 132, 146, 174
Rear Window 55 105, 171
Rebecca 48, 99
Redford, Robert 175
reframing 35, 37, 38, 122
Reville, Alma 176
Rio Bravo 56, 73
Rockwell, Norman 135
Rogen, Seth 113, 128
Rogers, Ginger 107
Room at the Top 108
Rope 55, 99, 154
Rosenberg, Julius and Ethel 101
Rota, Nino 155
Russell, Rosalind 107
Russo, Vito 98, 100

Sabotage 101
Saboteur 46, 55, 101, 147, 148
Sabrina 157
Sabu 170
Saint, Eva Marie 15, 53, 70, 85, 88, 90 102, 107, 108, 146, 147, 170, 173, 175, 181, 182
Satan Bug, The 131
Saturday Night Fever 111
Scorsese, Martin 168
Secret Agent 47, 101
Sergeant York 108
Seventh Veil, The 95
Shadow of a Doubt 15, 47, 48, 54, 55, 96, 99
Sheridan, Ann 107
Shining, The 168
Short Night, The 157
Shurlock, Geoffrey 182
Sidney, Sylvia 107
Siegel, Sol 181, 182
Smash-Up: The Story of a Woman 73
Somebody up There Likes Me 157
Some Like it Hot 108, 166
Sound of Music, The 157
Spartacus 168

Spoto, Daniel 91
Spy Who Came in from the Cold, The 103
Stage Fright 18, 48, 53, 154
Stanwyck, Barbara 109
Star is Born, A 95
Steiner, Max 155
Stewart, James 17, 45, 47, 89, 102, 105, 107, 108
Stranger at My Door 121
Strangers on a Train 15, 47, 48, 54, 78, 99
subjective camera 15, 42, 43, 46, 71, 87, 116, 117, 118, 122
Suddenly Last Summer 97
Sullivan, Jack 150, 151, 153, 154
surrealism 170
Suspicion 47, 53, 106
Sutton, Grady 98
Sweet Smell of Success 157-61

Talk of the Town, The 105
Tandy, Jessica 77
Tanguy, Yves 170
Tarantula 102
Tashlin, Frank 19
Taylor, Rod 18
Terminator, The 132
That Touch of Mink 25
Thief of Bagdad, The 170
Thin Man, The 73
39 Steps, The 14, 15, 46, 47, 55, 71, 101, 173
Thomson, David 95, 109
Three Days of the Condor 175
To Catch a Thief 54, 78, 105, 106, 107
Todd, Richard 18
Tomasini, George 15
Topaz 102, 103
Torn Curtain 102, 103, 108, 149
Torregrossa, Richard 112
Touch of Evil 115
Tourist, The 108
Travolta, John 111
Triesault, Ivan 50
Trouble with Harry, The 149
Truffaut, Francois 65, 94, 147, 175

Twentieth Century 166
Twentieth-Century Limited 13, 15, 21, 25, 29, 30, 33, 58, 65, 71, 75, 81, 83, 99 145, 164, 166, 179, 182
20,000 Leagues Under the Sea 95

Under Capricorn 48, 173
Under the Volcano 73
United Nations Building 35, 40, 41, 70, 71, 150, 152, 167, 168, 169, 174, 181

Valli, Alida 55
Van Sant, Gus 175
Vaughn, Robert 102
Velazquez, Diego 45, 48
Verdict, The 95
Vertigo 15, 16, 17, 42, 45, 54, 55, 56, 83, 105, 147, 149, 154, 168, 171, 176
View to a Kill, A 148

Wakefield, Dan 70
Walker, Robert 47, 78
Walk on the Wild Side 168

Way We Were, The 70
Welles, Orson 66
West, Mae 107
West Side Story 157, 168
White, Jacqueline 163, 164
Who's Afraid of Virginia Woolf? 157
Wilder, Billy 168
Wilder, Gene 175
Williams, William Carlos 53
Wilson, Sloan 111
Windsor, Marie 163, 164, 165
Wollen, Peter 63
Wright, Frank Lloyd 93, 167, 168
Wrong Man, The 14, 15, 55, 154
Wyman, Jane 18

Young, Loretta 107

Ziegfeld Follies 78

Bear Manor Media

Classic Cinema.
Timeless TV.
Retro Radio.

WWW.BEARMANORMEDIA.COM

www.ingramcontent.com/pod-product-compliance
Lightning Source LLC
Chambersburg PA
CBHW050926240426
43670CB00022B/2948